The Singer and the Song

# About the Author

Audrey Healy is a freelance journalist. Her work has been published in the *Sunday Independent, Ireland on Sunday, Roscommon Champion, Longford News, Westmeath Topic, NewsFour, Jemma Publications* and several other publications, including Dublin weeklies and trade magazines. A native of Rooskey, County Roscommon she has already published three books, *St Thérèse in Ireland, Dubliners: What's the Story?* and *Contacted* (co-written with Don Mullan).

She is a regular contributor to local radio and has recently begun songwriting with singer-songwriter Charlie McGettigan.

# The Singer and the Song

**Sixty Irish Songwriters and their Favourite Songs**

## AUDREY HEALY

HODDER
HEADLINE
IRELAND

First published in Ireland in 2006 by Hodder Headline Ireland
First published in Ireland in paperback in 2007 by
Hodder Headline Ireland

The right of Audrey Healy to be identified as the Author of the Work
has been asserted by her in accordance with the Copyright,
Designs and Patents Act 1988.

1

A CIP catalogue record for this title is available from the British Library

13-digit ISBN 978 0 340 92408 2

Typeset in Bembo by Anú Design, Tara
Cover and text design by Anú Design, Tara
Printed and bound in Great Britain by Clays Ltd, St Ives plc

Hodder Headline Ireland's policy is to use papers which are natural, renewable
and recyclable products and made from wood grown in sustainable forests.
The logging and manufacturing processes are expected to conform to
the environmental regulations of the country of origin.

Hodder Headline Ireland
8 Castlecourt Centre
Castleknock
Dublin 15
Ireland
A division of Hachette Livre UK Ltd,
338 Euston Road,
London, NW1 3BH

www.hhireland.ie

# Contents

## Indelible Memories

## The Loneliness of Loss

## Believe

## Sources of Love

## Inspiration

## A Song That Just Is

*For Emma, Alannah, Ciara, Billy and Cian...*
*you arrived just in time!*

*Also dedicated to the memory of Lisa Bassett. This is for you.*

# *Foreword*

Audrey Healy represents exactly the sort of person Brainwave needs out in the community: someone who is not prepared to let her epilepsy get in the way of achieving the ambitions she has set for herself, and someone who is living as full a life as possible while recognising that her lifestyle has to be tailored, just a little bit, because of the condition. Audrey, as the successful author of three books, as a journalist who has contributed to most of the top Irish newspapers, as a poet and as a songwriter, ticks all the boxes in what we look for, so she was pushing an open door when she asked us to support her in her latest book project. Apart from that reason, the number of prominent singer-songwriters who have epilepsy is quite high. Some, like Neil Young who has had epilepsy since childhood, are very open about this, but one of the UK's best-known international singer-songwriters threatened Epilepsy Action, the UK's biggest epilepsy charity, with legal action if they ever mentioned his epilepsy again. So, even in the arts world, the disclosure of epilepsy can be clouded with stigma. This is why Brainwave is always looking for role models for people with epilepsy, especially younger people, to look up to and help them to be more open about their condition.

When I read *Dubliners: What's the Story?*, I was struck by how eclectic the mix of people Audrey had included in her book was; she seemed to ignore any ground rules for who might be eligible for inclusion. Instead, she went with her instinct and included anybody connected to the city who she found interesting. It is precisely this varied mix of Dubliners which makes the book work. The reader turns from reading about some 17th-century religious figure on one page to find a modern-day radio presenter on the next. It seems too that Audrey has followed this instinct again with *The Singer and the Song*. Once again, she was not tempted to stick rigidly to some genre of music or style of singing but has sought out all manner of songs from all types of songwriters and singers. Ultimately, it seems that although the song and the singer and the songwriter are all very important, it's the story of the song that ties everything together, and it is this story that Audrey has gone after. Using her own experience of writing songs combined with her journalist's nose for a story, Audrey Healy has produced a winning combination that should ensure that *The Singer and the Song* becomes a major success story for Audrey. All of us here at Brainwave, the Irish Epilepsy Association, are very proud of our association with Audrey, and people with epilepsy everywhere can take immense pride in her achievements.

*Mike Glynn, CEO of Brainwave*
*July 2006*

# *Introduction*

As every picture tells a story, each song we hear carries its own history, and the journey from the original idea to the final production can bring the author through many bright and dark alleyways in an attempt to reach that moment when the song is declared finished and ready for the listening ear. There are no set rules and there is no specific format. All you require as a writer is an audience of at least one, other than yourself, who is moved in some shape or form by the result of your efforts. Some songs take little time to write, while others can take years to reach completion. A good song will affect people in various ways. It will relate to different emotions, occasions, triumphs, failures, love, life, death, victory or loss. A good song can cross generations, religions, continents, languages and culture. Songwriting is a beautiful and privileged art form with great rewards. A hit song will open so many doors for its creator and performer, offering lucrative financial opportunities and the possibility of good solid financial security.

This book invites the reader into the creative music world, giving you an insight into the relationship between the artist and the work. Some of these songs are instantly recognisable. Some are national treasures indelibly etched in our psyche. In some cases, this will be your first introduction to a song. You will be treated to some fine anecdotes relating to the writing, recording and/or performance of particular songs.

I hope you enjoy the read and I hope it adds to your day. It is my privilege to be associated with this project and to be surrounded by so many great songwriters and artists. My greatest respect is reserved for Audrey Healy who had a really interesting idea to help her in her quest to highlight the condition of epilepsy here in Ireland.

*Mike Hanrahan, Chairman of IMRO*
*July 2006*

# *Preface and Acknowledgements*

Coffee shops seem to be the places to go for literary inspiration – my last book, *Contacted*, was conjured up in Bewley's Café on Westmoreland Street in the company of co-author Don Mullan, and *The Singer and the Song* was tentatively born out of a similar brainstorming session in Starbucks Café in Dublin. This book was something of a whirlwind for me and arose, quite accidentally, as a result of a couple of short conversations I had with two of the book's contributors, in the course of my work as a journalist with a provincial newspaper. Ironically, the artists in question, who both feature in this book, are connected in a way – Brendan Graham is the composor of 'Rock 'N' Roll Kids', while it was Charlie McGettigan who, along with Paul Harrington, scooped first prize in the 1994 Eurovision Song Contest performing Brendan's song.

I had always loved the nostalgic yet simple lyrics of 'Rock 'N' Roll Kids' and was curious to know how the song had come about. Brendan's tale of its origin, combined with an earlier conversation I had had with Charlie about one of his compositions 'Feet Of A Dancer' fused together and got me thinking about the many different stories behind so many different songs.

And so I set out to find those writers and find those stories. I found songs born out of love, songs born out of jealousy, loss and humour, but in all the musicians I found an eagerness to participate in the project and a genuine passion for music and for the role it has played in their lives.

•

This book, quite simply, would not exist without the generosity and assistance of a number of very special people, and I would like to gratefully acknowledge their kindness here. First, to Don, with whom I first shared this idea; his response was instantly receptive, and his enthusiasm was instrumental in my decision to forge ahead with the project.

A number of the artists featured in this book must be singled out for the extra time they gave me in the course of its compilation. Charlie McGettigan, as someone I have recently begun writing songs with, was one of the first on my list of contributors. He was enthusiastic from the beginning and helped me enormously with contacts.

Second, Diarmuid O'Leary from The Bards, who has put up with me now for over fifteen years and who, when he wasn't in the studio recording yet another album, was on the other end of the phone and was a wonderful – and always entertaining – source of information.

However, top marks must go to Mike Hanrahan whom I first met when we were both on the judging panel of the An Tostal song contest in Drumshanbo, County Leitrim, in May 2005. As Chairman of IMRO, he was my first contact for many of the high-profile names featured in *The Singer and the Song,* and, from the moment I contacted him, he was excited about the project and able and willing to help in any way he could. He was very much instrumental in helping me to secure interviews with many of the top names listed in this book.

I'd like to thank the many singers and songwriters from all corners of Ireland and beyond who responded to my appeal for interviews with both speed and eagerness. You will note that the cover specifically says Irish songwriters, but I have broken the rules somewhat and included a couple of UK-born singer-songwriters who have formed a deep and lasting connection with the Emerald Isle, most notably Charlie Landsborough, Hazel O'Connor and Eric Bogle.

The list of contributors is long and varied, from Christy Moore to Christie Hennessy, Niamh Kavanagh to Nina Hynes, Declan Nerney to Don Baker, and I am delighted that so many of these busy performers should have taken time out of their hectic schedules to be a part of this publication. I hope their generous contributions will make it a feast of delight for you, the reader, and that amongst the selection of songs featured you will find one that means something special to you.

I chose Brainwave, the Irish Epilepsy Association as the recipient for part of the royalties earned from this book because I have had epilepsy since I had a brain tumour when I was fifteen. The consequences of living with the condition are as individual as those who have it, and, like many others, I am on daily medication and try to avoid situations whereby I might be more susceptible to a seizure, things like late nights, too much computer work, stress or alcohol.

When I first developed epilepsy, I admit that I knew nothing about it. After dealing with the practical side of it and being prescribed medication, my next port of call was learning to accept it as a part of me, and that's where Brainwave came into its own. Both the organisation and what it stands for are focused on what you can do rather than what you can't. Of course, there are obstacles to overcome in your day-to-day life, but it is still possible to lead a happy and fulfilled life with epilepsy, and it certainly hasn't stopped me doing what I want to do – and that's writing.

A couple of years ago, Brainwave ran a competition for a trip to Finland and I emerged as one of the lucky winners. Together with three other young Irish women, I set off on an adventure-filled three-week long excursion. When we reached our destination in Helsinki, we were teamed up with our German, French and Finnish counterparts, and, together, we talked about the condition that had brought us together – our epilepsy – and the way in which it affected our lives. What I remember most about that trip are all the positives – the fact that we stayed all out all night camping and canoeing, the field trips, the rock-climbing, things I might never have had the courage to do at home because of the fear of having a seizure, but there, in Finland, every exercise was medically supervised and we were all equal. We came away from those weeks stronger and more confident people.

Brainwave were the first to run a course of this kind in Ireland for people with epilepsy. It's called Training for Success and is based in the Sligo Institute of Technology and is specifically aimed at people with epilepsy. Modules include art and media, computers and health and fitness, and students are encouraged to be positive about their epilepsy.

*Epilepsy News* is an informative publication which is distributed free to members of Brainwave and keeps them up to date with all that is happening in the world of epilepsy: advances in medicine, educational articles, interviews and regional news. In addition to the head office in Dublin, there are regional offices in Sligo, Galway, Tullamore, Limerick, Dundalk, Letterkenny, Kilkenny, Tralee and Cork.

Brainwave offer both emotional support and practical help to those with epilepsy – from concerned parents, teachers and guardians, to frightened teenagers on the brink of adulthood, who may see the condition as an obstacle in their journey towards independent adulthood. They help people deal with the practical implications one might face as a result of the condition, providing invaluable advice on issues relating to basic first aid – what to do in the event of a seizure – trigger factors, getting a driving licence, employment issues, insurance, entitlements, as well as providing specialist aids and appliances such as safety pillows and identity bracelets, which may well prove to be a lifeline when someone has a seizure. Earlier this year, Brainwave launched a brand new web site which is up to date and user-friendly. If you have epilepsy or know someone who has and would like some help or advice, you can access all their services and more at www.epilepsy.ie.

I personally believe that epilepsy is a condition which still, wrongly, has a stigma attached to it. Because of the way it manifests itself, it is not talked about as openly as illnesses such as asthma or diabetes, and, ironically, people with epilepsy are dependant on such openness. If I have a seizure, it is in my interests that the person next to me knows exactly what to do, and, if it is never spoken about, how will we ever overcome these obstacles?

Shortly after I decided to write this book, I set up a meeting with Mike Glynn, the Chief Executive Officer of Brainwave, and, after a little over half an hour of talking – and with the project still very much in its infancy – he readily and without hesitation agreed to become involved in the venture. His confident and buoyant response to the idea was a refreshing one and spurred me on to secure a deal.

Similarly, within a week of first approaching Hodder Headline Ireland with this idea, a meeting had been set up and *The Singer and the Song* was born. From Day One, Claire Rourke, Ciara Considine and Ciara Doorley have been a pleasure to work with, and I would like to thank them for all the work they have carried out behind the scenes to bring this beautiful book to fruition. I hope they are as proud of it as I am.

I would like to thank Adrienne Murphy and Joe Finnegan for contacts and Seamus Cashman for his invaluable support and advice and for the gift of the title of the book (albeit inadvertently!). I would also like to thank my brother Paul, for proofreading and editorial advice and Michael Whyte for technical assistance.

I'd also like to thank County Longford Librarian Mary Carletron Reynolds, Kitty Rodgers and all the staff of Longford Library for their kindness and support; the staff of the *Longford News and*, finally Thomas, Paul, Liam and Mark and my parents, Rutledge and May, and my friends, for their patience and support in this project.

I hope the music in this book brings you to where you want to be. Enjoy.

*Audrey Healy*
*Longford, July 2006*

# Indelible Memories

## Diarmuid O'Leary — The Bards

### Lanigan's Ball

*Old Traditional Song*

*Taken from the album* The Best of Diarmuid O'Leary and The Bards

Around 1975, I drove on to the ferry at Holyhead after doing a few gigs in London, and Christy Moore pulled up behind me on the car deck. Naturally, we headed to the bar and, on the journey to Dún Laoghaire, we reminisced and chatted about the music – over quite a few brandies! Christy taught me 'Lanigan's Ball' and suggested that I do a version. He told me it was an old traditional song, which he originally found in Colm O'Lochlainn's book *Irish Street Ballads*.

Over a period of time, I dabbled with the song and discovered it was very long and quite a mouthful to learn.

At the time, The Bards consisted of Ann O'Connor, Christy Sheridan and myself, and one night we were playing for Mick McCarthy in The Embankment in Tallaght, County Dublin. The Embankment was the venue of the day for folk music and where many of us started off and played regularly.

We were in the middle of the show and half of the sound system cut out and all our instruments went off the air. We were left with only one microphone working. When something like that happens on stage, a silence descends and for a few seconds nobody knows what to do. I don't know why, but I suddenly broke into, 'In the town of Athy, one Jeremy Lanigan… '. I nodded at Ann to pick up the bodhrán to help me out. Here and there, I forgot the words, so to cover up I gave a running commentary on how Ann should hold the stick and keep rhythm on the bodhrán. A lot of banter ensued, and, out of nothing, a very humorous item developed live on stage. It was obvious that the audience took to the song instantly, and Mick McCarthy came on stage and said it was a pity that the sound didn't break down every night. After the show, the song was the main talking point, and I remember Mick saying, 'O'Leary, you have to learn that song and get it into the show!' From that accidental performance I knew the song had a lot of potential.

When I got home that night, I got out the words, and, while reading through all the verses, I discovered the character 'Julia at the Ball'. It dawned on me that this could be a great duet for myself and Ann, with her becoming 'Julia', playing the bodhrán and stepping it out with a reel or a jig. It was then that I started to learn the song seriously as a duet with Ann. It was included in every live show from there on and developed nightly, with spontaneous comments and banter about Julia, her bodhrán-playing and her dancing routine. It instantly became the most popular song in the show, lasting anything up to ten minutes depending on what happened on the night. Audiences continually asked if we were recording it, as it was bound to be a hit.

Coincidentally, through this period, we had been recording our first album on which all the material was of a serious folk nature. Because of the feedback we were getting to the song in the live shows, and even though it was out of context, we decided to record it and include it on the album. I asked Bill Whelan to produce the recording as I was impressed with the work he was doing with some of the best folk and traditional artists at the time, including Planxty whom he joined for a period. Bill came to a live show, and, after seeing the performance of the song, he felt it was best to record it just as it was performed on stage – banter and all. I invited Peadar

Mercier, who played bodhrán with The Chieftains, to join us on the recording. When we recorded the first take of the song, Bill asked us to come into the control room to have a listen, and I remember Peadar saying, 'Gentlemen, you've just heard a classic, that's it, leave it alone!' Little did I know at the time what phenomenal success Bill Whelan would enjoy fifteen years later when he composed the music for the now internationally famous *Riverdance*.

The record company selected 'Song for a Winter's Night' as the first single from the album and put 'Lanigan's Ball' on the B-side. At the time, Mike Murphy was the host of the early morning show on RTÉ Radio One, and he started to play 'Lanigan's Ball' regularly. He got huge reaction to it, and the single was re-released with 'Lanigan's Ball' on the A-side. It became one of Ireland's biggest-selling singles, giving us our first hit song and earning gold discs for both the single and the album.

I owe this song a lot and still enjoy singing it and 'steppin' it out' after all these years. Thanks to Christy Moore for the start!

## Lanigan's Ball

*In the town of Athy one Jeremy Lanigan*
*Battered away till he hadn't a pound*
*His father he died and made him a man again,*
*Left him a farm and ten acres of ground*
*He gave a grand party to friends and relations*
*Who didn't forget him when come to the wall*
*If you but listen, I'll make your eyes glisten*
*At rows and ructions at Lanigan's Ball*

### Chorus
*Six long months I spent in Dublin*
*Six long months doing nothing at all*
*Six long months I spent in Dublin*
*Learning to dance for Lanigan's Ball*
*I stepped out and she stepped in again  (x3)*

*Learning to dance for Lanigan's Ball*
*Myself to be sure got free invitations*
*For all the nice girls and boys I might ask*
*Just in a minute both friends and relations*
*Were dancing as merry as bees round a cask*

*There was lashings of punch and wine for the ladies*
*Potatoes and cakes, there was bacon and tea*
*There were the Nolans, the Dolans, O'Gradys*
*Courting the girls and dancing away*

*They were doing all kinds of nonsensical polkas*
*All round the room in a whirly gig*
*Till Julia and I soon banished their nonsense*
*And tipped them a twist of a real Irish jig*

*Oh how that girl she got mad on me*
*We danced till you'd think the ceilings would fall*
*For I'd spent three weeks at Brooks Academy*
*Learning the steps for Lanigan's Ball*

***Chorus***
*Six long months I spent in Dublin*
*Six long months doing nothing at all*
*Six long months I spent in Dublin*
*Learning to dance for Lanigan's Ball*
*I stepped out and she stepped in again (x3)*
*Learning to dance for Lanigan's Ball*

*The boys were as merry, the girls all hearty*
*Dancing together in couples and groups*
*Till an accident happened, young Terence McCarthy*
*He put his right leg through Miss Finerty's hoops*

*The creature she fainted and cried 'Meelia Murther'*
*Called for her brothers and gathered them all*
*Carmody swore that he'd go no further,*
*He'd have satisfaction at Lanigan's Ball*

*In the midst of the row Miss Kerrigan fainted*
*Her cheeks at the same time as red as the rose*
*Some of the boys decreed she was painted*
*She took a small drop too much I suppose*

*Her sweetheart Ned Morgan so powerful and able*
*When he saw his fair cailín stretched by the wall*
*He tore the left leg from under the table*
*And smashed all the dishes at Lanigan's Ball*

**Chorus**
*Six long months I spent in Dublin*
*Six long months doing nothing at all*
*Six long months I spent in Dublin*
*Learning to dance for Lanigan's Ball*
*I stepped out and she stepped in again (x3)*
*Learning to dance for Lanigan's Ball*

*Boys, oh boys, tis then there was ructions*
*I took a lick from young Phelim McHugh*
*But soon I replied to his fine introduction*
*And kicked him a terrible hullabaloo*

*Auld Casey the piper he nearly got strangled*
*They squeezed up his pipes, bellows, chanters and all*
*The girls in their ribbons they all got entangled*
*And that put an end to Lanigan's Ball*

**Repeat Chorus**

# BIOGRAPHY

Diarmuid O'Leary was born in Rosslare, County Wexford, one of a family of three, with a brother Tom and a sister Margaret. His mother was from the fishing village of Fethard-on-Sea on the Hook Peninsula, and all his summers as a child and into adulthood were spent there, with her family, the Molloys and the Dillons. His father was from Limerick and was one of the first recruits to the Garda Síochaná when the force was founded in 1922. Diarmuid's father was transferred to the village of Paulstown in County Kilkenny when Diarmuid was two years old, and the family stayed there until they moved to Dublin when Diarmuid was eighteen.

Growing up in Paulstown, there was no great tradition of music in the house. In fact, musical instruments were scarce in the area so the songs Diarmuid heard on the radio – irrespective of style – were his main interest and influence. He listened to Elvis Presley and Buddy Holly, country singers like Don Gibson and Jim Reeves, the great crooners Bing Crosby and Frank Sinatra and the sound of the electric guitar with Les Paul, and, later, Hank Marvin and The Shadows, the skiffle style of Lonnie Donegan, and then on to the whole folk revival with Pete Seegar, The Clancy Brothers & Tommy Makem, right up to The Beatles and Bob Dylan.

It was his relationship with his two uncles Sonny and Jim Molloy in Fethard-on-Sea, however, that facilitated Diarmuid's apprenticeship in the entertainment business. Both were great characters and loved to sing a song and tell a story. From an early age, he used to join in with them at family gatherings, and, as he got older, the three became great friends and teamed up for regular sessions in the pubs in the village and surrounding areas.

In the early 1960s, Diarmuid was a regular contributor at parties in Dublin, and it was during this time that he was introduced to Billy Watson, who had just retired as the bandleader of the orchestra in Clery's Ballroom. Billy was looking for a singer/guitarist to start a new group to perform in pubs, and Diarmuid successfully auditioned. Together with Billy's son Neville, they began performing together – the first time he got paid for singing.

Diarmuid gradually became more interested in folk music and ballads, and one night while performing at a function in Dublin he met Pat Ryan, a musician from County Clare. They teamed up for a few songs and found that they performed well together. They started rehearsing, became a duo on the folk circuit and adopted the name The Bards, playing regularly in the Embankment in Tallaght.

Over the next few years, the line-up of the group changed several times. Along the way, Diarmuid and Pat discovered a female vocalist, Ann O'Connor, who later became 'Julia'. In the late 1970s, Pat decided to drop out of the group, and Diarmuid and Ann were joined by Christy Sheridan, playing mandolin and banjo.

In 1980, they released the single, Lanigan's Ball, which became one of Ireland's biggest-selling singles, giving them their first hit song and earning gold discs for both the album and the single. The group was later joined by Fran Curry and enjoyed further success with 'The Oldest Swinger In Town'. 'Smithy', Michael Smith, joined the band around this time, playing electric and double bass. Today, The Bards feature Diarmuid, Christy Sheridan and Smithy.

In the past few years, Diarmuid has spent a lot of time in the studio, recording new material and tidying up the back catalogue, producing and arranging the songs jointly with his friend Peter Eades, who is a very talented musician and studio engineer. New recordings include *The Finest*, *Classic Comedy Hits*, *The Railway Hotel*, *The Final Curtain: Live from Clontarf Castle* and *The Early Years*.

Michael McLoughlin

*Brendan Graham*

## Rock 'N' Roll Kids

*Written by Brendan Graham*

March 1990, we crowded in – us white-boys in suits and ties – fresh from the offices and counting houses of Dublin. Crowded in to the sweat of the National Boxing Stadium. Blood had been spilt here. Now, tonight, on the fight stage of the South Circular Road, it was the Fat Man from N' Orleans pumpin' out the sounds of the Deep South – New Orleans, where the Swamp Irish had once gone in the 1800s – dug out the bayous, wrassled with alligators and fought against the Irish of the North to preserve the Republic of Slavery.

Now tonight, the music took us somewhere over there – 'Walkin' To New Orleans' ... 'Blueberry Hill' ... 'Jambalaya' – the Irish stew of the Mississippi. On stage, 'Fats' Antoine Domino was stewin' up a storm between the walking bass of the piano and the Dixie horns blasting us out of our seats. We'd never be white no more, 'Niggers turned inside out' was what we were, just like the Yankee Nativists used to call us Irish back in the days of the American Civil War. Then, we slaughtered each other in their war – died our way into their affections – died to become white. Tonight, we would be black again.

The apprentice accountants and the young-buck lawyers loosened their ties, left their seats and bopped in the aisles. They had been freed, the flimsy skin of conservatism flung from them like a Clery's-best suit jacket. The *domino* effect. It was one of those moments of absolute clarity – like a knock-out punch. I begged the pen of an accountant beside me. A Parker – with a real nib. I hadn't a stitch of paper, only the crumpled up, half-ticket that had ushered me in. Lilac, with numbers on it … just enough space for a title – 'Rock 'N' Roll Kids'! Coopers-&-Lybrand-man awaited anxiously for the return of his Parker.

'Rock 'N' Roll Kids', I said to myself. 'Underneath, that's what we all are.' I didn't write the song straight away. When I did write it, I wanted to keep that theme – that somehow in our hearts we are always sixteen. Then we get trussed up by life – never seem to rock 'n' roll anymore.

Ken Stewart, an old friend and astute songman, came to visit me. I played him all four verses and three choruses I'd written. It was six minutes long. He kindheartedly said, 'You have the "makings" of a hit song there.' So I chewed at it until the meat was gone and only the bone was left.

What to do with it then? I didn't sing, and who was there in Ireland doing that bittersweet slice-of-life type song? The Eurovision Song Contest still held some modicum of cachet in the early 1990s, but it wasn't a Eurovision song either. But then, I wondered, wouldn't it be something to submit a song that had no bells, bugles or belly-dancing … just a song, and let it stand or let it fall on its own merits?

I entered it once; I entered it twice, and, against all sound advice, I entered it thrice. I believed in the song and had re-demoed it very simply, with Paul Harrington on vocals and piano. I loved the intimacy Paul created for the story. At last, it got selected for the National Song Contest. I wanted to keep it small, but was piano and voice just too small? I had a hunch that Charlie McGettigan's voice would work well with Paul's, and his gentle guitar style would underscore the piano. Tentatively, I made the suggestion: would they perform the song together? To my everlasting gratitude, they both agreed. There would be no arrangement, no band, no orchestra, no backing singers – nothing except two great storytellers on piano and guitar. It would be a conversation in a kitchen … albeit a kitchen with a vast television audience.

The first time it got an airing on *Kenny Live*, presenter Pat Kenny took me aside and said, 'If that song doesn't win the whole darn thing I'll eat my hat!' 'Rock 'N' Roll Kids' subsequently did go on to win the 1994 Eurovision Song Contest by one of the biggest margins in the history of the contest and became the only purely acoustic song to ever do so.

Pat Kenny's hat remained suitably intact.

A pity!

### Rock 'N' Roll Kids

*I remember '62,*
*I was sixteen and so were you,*
*And we lived next door,*
*On the avenue;*
*Jerry Lee was big and Elvis too,*
*Blue jeans and blue suede shoes,*
*And we never knew what life held in store,*
*We just wanted to Rock 'n' Roll forever more.*

*We were the Rock 'n' Roll Kids,*
*Rock 'n' Roll was all we did,*
*And listening to those songs*
*On the radio;*
*I was yours and you were mine,*
*That was once upon a time,*
*Now we never seem to Rock 'n' Roll*
*Anymore.*

*Now Johnny's in love with the girl next door,*
*And Mary's down at the record store,*
*They don't want to be … around us no more;*
*'Golden Oldies' but we hardly speak,*
*Too busy running to a different beat,*
*Hard to understand, we were once like them;*
*How I wish we could find,*
*Those Rock 'n' Roll days again.*

*We were the Rock 'n' Roll Kids*
*Rock 'n' roll was all we did,*
*And listening to those songs,*
*On the radio;*
*I was yours and you were mine,*
*That was once upon a time,*
*Now we never seem to Rock 'n' Roll…*

*We just never seem to Rock 'n' Roll*
*Anymore.*

## BIOGRAPHY

A native of County Tipperary, Brendan Graham is a novelist and songwriter. He has had songs recorded by a diverse group of artists, from *sean-nós* singer Róisín Elsafty and Capercaillie's Karen Matheson to New York Metropolitan Opera leading soprano Young Ok Shin, as well as by Secret Garden, Dervish, Brian Kennedy, Sissel, Russell Watson, Ronan Tynan, The Irish Tenors, Celtic Woman, Tommy Fleming, Seán Keane, Daniel O'Donnell, Anúna and Il Divo. His song 'You Raise Me Up' (music by Rolf Lovland) became a No. 1 hit in the USA for Christian group Selah and was also the No. 1 single from Josh Groban's multi-platinum album *Closer,* with the singer's performance of the song garnering a 2005 Grammy nomination. The song then went on to become No. 1 in Ireland and Record of the Year in the UK for Westlife.

With over 120 recordings by some of the world's leading artists, 'You Raise Me Up' has become a modern-day classic.

In 2005, Brendan was shortlisted for Songwriter of the Year and Song of the Year at the Gospel Music Awards in Nashville. He was also the recipient of *Irish Music Magazine*'s Songwriter Award.

He is the author of *The Whitest Flower* (Harper Collins), a documentary novel on Ireland's Great Famine, which received widespread international acclaim and went to No. 2 in the Irish best-seller list, as well as being translated into a number of languages. *The Element of Fire* followed in 2001, while *The Brightest Day, The Darkest Night* a novel of the Irish in the American Civil War – was published in paperback in November 2006. *The Whitest Flower* and *The Element of Fire* both form part of the recommended 'support fiction' for Ireland's new, Leaving Certificate History Syllabus 2006.

His songs, the aforementioned 'Rock 'N' Roll Kids' (1994) and 'The Voice' (1996), performed by Eimear Quinn, were Ireland's last two winning songs in the Eurovision Song Contest. 'Rock 'N' Roll Kids' was recently voted by RTÉ's *Late Late Show* viewers as their favourite Irish Eurovision song of all time.

Brendan was Chairman of IMRO, the Irish Music Rights Organisation, for a nine-year period until 1997, during which time he was appointed to FORTE, the government task force to develop Ireland's music industry. In 1999, he was the recipient of the inaugural IMRO Award, at which Taoiseach Bertie Ahern cited Graham's outstanding contribution to Ireland's music industry. Brendan currently lives in County Mayo.

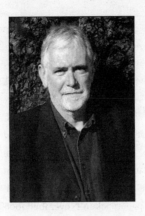

*Charlie McGettigan*

## A Bed For The Night

*Written by Charlie McGettigan*

*Taken from the album Charlie McGettigan*

It was a wet and windy November night as we pulled up outside the St Brendan's Irish Centre in Manchester. There were about forty of us on the bus – singers, musicians, dancers, storytellers and road crew – and this was the first gig of our concert tour called A Taste of Leitrim. The tour was organised by a bunch of us who lived in Drumshanbo, County Leitrim, to raise funds to buy a large hall in the town called the Mayflower Ballroom, and convert it into a community centre. It was the 1980s, and money was scarce, so we thought we'd try the tour to see if we could prise a few pounds from the Leitrim diaspora in England.

In Manchester, we were to meet Fr. John Aherne, whose parochial house was close to the centre, to gain admittance to the venue, but, on arrival, there was no sign of him. The rain was pounding off the Manchester streets as we huddled on the bus. I was near the front of the bus when I heard a knocking on the passenger entrance door. Our driver opened the door and standing outside with his hair plastered to his head and his light grey suit soaked was a tall thin young man of about twenty-one or twenty-two years of age.

'Would ye know if Fr. John Aherne would be about the place?' said the forlorn stranger in a broad Meath accent. 'Someone told me he lived here.'

Our driver told him that we were hoping to meet him here ourselves and that hopefully he'd be here soon.

'I lost me wallet on the train coming down from Liverpool', said the young man, 'and all me money and addresses was in it.'

Our driver, thinking that this was a bit of a sob story, told him how sorry he was to hear that, and just then a car pulled up outside the centre. A tall man of about thirty-five years of age in casual clothes got out and came towards the bus.

'You'd be the Leitrim crowd I suppose', he said in a lovely, lilting Kerry accent.

'You're early – I'm John Aherne. I'll let ye in now, and who's this?' He was talking to the tall, thin stranger.

'I'm Willy Gurk,' said the stranger. 'I'm from Oldcastle, County Meath, and someone told me at the railway station that you might be able to help me.'

'Come on in,' said Fr. John, 'and we'll see what we can do.'

We all trooped out of the bus and into the old community hall that was St Brendan's Irish Centre. Instruments and amplification were unloaded and soon the heat was on in the hall and tea was being made. Willy and Fr. John were deep in conversation, but we could all hear the chat clearly.

'Stockton, you say? Your uncle is John Gurk and he lives in Stockton?' Fr. John was asking.

Soon the big parish record books were out and phone calls were being made. In the space of half an hour, contact was made with Willy's uncle and arrangements were made for his collection.

Our concert turned out to be a great success, but, for me, the highlight was that simple act of kindness done by John Aherne on that cold November night in the tough times of the 1980s. The incident inspired me to write 'A Bed For The Night', which I still perform to this day, and I always think of John Aherne and Willy Gurk as I sing it.

This song featured on *Rock 'N' Roll Kids: The Album* by Paul Harrington and Charlie McGettigan and was also a single for Dublin band Allies. It also appeared on the album *Helpless Heart* by Maura O'Connell.

## A Bed For The Night

*He was standing on the corner as the sun was going down.*
*He was looking for a contact, he had just arrived in town.*
*With his suitcase full of emptiness, his clothes outworn and tight,*
*He was looking for a bed for the night.*

*And he had a list of numbers that had slipped out of his head,*
*An uncle living somewhere out in Manchester he said.*
*He had come out of a country where the tunnels had no lights,*
*And he was looking for a bed for the night.*

### Chorus
*Just a bed for the night, somewhere warm till the morning light,*
*He was looking for a bed for the night.*

*And standing in the doorway was a man called Father John.*
*He said, 'Come in from the cold and sit you down there my good man'*
*And the small talk was of football, and the tea tasted so right,*
*When he was looking for a bed for the night.*

### Chorus
*Just a bed for the night, somewhere warm till the morning light,*
*He was looking for a bed for the night.*

*There was something in this situation, made me realise,*
*That there is always someone with a kindness in their eyes.*
*So if Father John should hear me, and who knows? He just might,*
*Hear me say, 'Thank you for the bed for the night.'*

**Chorus**
*Just a bed for the night, somewhere warm till the morning light,*
*He was looking for a bed for the night.*

## BIOGRAPHY

Charlie McGettigan started his musical career in the 1960s, heavily influenced by artists like The Beatles, The Rolling Stones and all the high-profile names of that period. In 1968, Charlie moved to Dublin and honed in on the thriving folk scene there at that time. His influences were people like Paul Brady, Dónal Lunny and Andy Irvine. Having played electric guitar up to then, he purchased his first acoustic guitar and concentrated on developing the finger-picking style, which is now his stock in trade.

Moving to the rural environment of Drumshanbo, County Leitrim, in 1973, Charlie formed the highly successful Jargon group, which went on to win the prestigious Letterkenny Folk Festival, which in turn, led to a recording contract with Polygram records and the release of Jargon's first single 'Bailieboro And Me'. The band went on to record two more singles before Charlie left to pursue a solo career.

Over the following years, he released two solo albums before joining forces with Paul Harrington and Brendan Graham to win the 1994 Eurovision Song Contest with 'Rock 'N' Roll Kids'. He subsequently recorded *Rock 'N' Roll Kids The Album* with Paul Harrington, but the duo went their separate ways shortly after its release in 1994.

Charlie has since pursued a solo career, releasing the albums *In Your Old Room* and *Family Matters*. He tours extensively, both here and abroad, and his songs have been recorded by many other artists, including Dé Danann, Mary Black and Frances Black, Ray Lynam, Daniel O'Donnell, Hal Ketchum, Maura O'Connell and Eleanor Shanley.

Down the years, Charlie has made many television appearances both in Ireland and further afield and has presented his own television and radio specials for RTÉ and the BBC. He currently has his own weekly radio programme on Shannonside Radio.

In November 2005, Charlie travelled to Nashville, Tennessee, to work with the legendary producer Bil VornDick, and recorded fourteen tracks for a new album, *Stolen Moments*, which was released in August 2006. Top acoustic musicians Randy Kohrs (dobro), Aubrie Hainie (fiddle/mandolin), Mark Fain (bass), Pete Huttlinger (guitars), Sam Levine (clarinet), Pat McInerney (drums/percussion), Patti Mitchell (vocals) and Chip Davis (vocals) participated in the recordings over a four-day live session. The album contains new songs by Charlie and some written in collaboration with other writers.

*John Spillane*

## Gortatagort

*Written by John Spillane*

*Yet to be released*

'Gortatagort' is the name of my uncle's farm near Bantry in West Cork where I spent nearly all my holidays – Christmas, Easter and summer – from the age of four until I was about seventeen.

There were about 40 acres of a farm, some good land and some bad; all the fields had names, many of which were in Irish. My father died when myself and my four brothers were very young, so it was a great break for my mother when we were bundled onto the Bantry bus at holiday time. We loved the farm and considered ourselves to be half-country and half-city children.

Life was very different on the farm, and we worked hard saving the hay, cleaning out the stalls, going for the cows and saving the turf from the bog. I saw a whole way of life disappear during those years.

When I was small, there used to be cows, calves, heifers, bullocks, hay, barley, rushes, hens, bees, the sow, *banbhs*, the mare, the foal, the plough, the turf, the spuds, parsnips, cabbage, carrots, etc. The only farming that goes on there now is dry cattle. I sing this song in praise of the farm, and I dedicate it to my Uncle Tim, who passed away in 2005.

## Gortatagort

*I sing the fields, I sing the farm.*
*I sing the house my mother was born,*
*In Gortatagort, Colomane,*
*A green jewel,*

*Sewn in a patchwork quilt of fields,*
*Between the mountain and the river,*
*In this time now and in another,*

*Where I ran free with my brothers,*
*Through the long meadow, the Cnocán Rua,*
*The fort field, the Páirc na Claise,*
*The new house field, the gallán field,*
*The clover field, the rushy field,*

*Where the red fuschia weeps in the hen's garden,*
*And the angels bleed over Bantry Bay,*

*I see the house, I see the yard,*
*I see the stall, I see the stable,*
*I see the haggard and the hen's garden,*
*I see the hill, I see the well,*

*I sing the spring and the well water,*
*The flat field, the hilly field,*
*The South Ray grass, the North Ray grass,*
*The brake and the Páircín na Heornan,*

*Where the red fuschia weeps in the hen's garden,*
*And God goes to sleep in the hills and valleys,*
*And the moon rises over the haggard,*
*And peace descends on Gortatagort,*
*And the angels bleed over Bantry Bay,*

*Ah saddle up the old grey mare,*
*Tim Big Danny and Jackie Timmy,*
*Are gonna ride across the mountains to Puck Fair*

*I sing the fields I sing the farm,*
*I sing the house my mother was born,*
*In Gortatagort, Colomane,*
*A green jewel.*

## BIOGRAPHY

It is not hard to fathom when you hear that soft lilt that John Spillane is a Cork man – and a proud one at that. He's even been quoted as describing the county of his birth as 'the centre of the universe' – and one suspects he's not joking!

It's been said that John's voice is one 'full of honesty, commitment and sensitivity', and this is certainly evident in his debut solo album *The Wells of the World,* released in 1997.

Prior to setting out on his own, John played for a number of years with The Stargazers and enjoyed a subsequent stint with Nomos.

His second album, *Will We Be Brilliant Or What?* entered the Irish album charts at No. 14 and was produced by Peter O'Toole (The Hothouse Flowers) and Declan Sinnott.

Professionally, 2003 was a good year for the affable singer-songwriter with a number of talented Irish musicians choosing to record his songs, including Christy Moore, Sharon Shannon, Seán Keane and Karen Casey, while up-and-coming star George Murphy's first single was a John Spillane composition

'The Moon Going Home'; it reached No. 2 in the Irish charts and remained there for two weeks.

John himself picked up the prestigious Meteor Ireland Music Award in the Best Folk/Traditional Act category in 2003.

The year 2004 brought more success as John produced and performed on a Brown Bag Films animation (who also produced the award-nominated *Give Up Your Auld Sins* animation) called *The Boy Who Had No Story,* which was based on one of John's songs, 'What's The Story Rory'. This won IFTAs (Irish Film and Television Awards) under two categories: Best Animation and Best Children's Programme.

When Cork was christened European Capital of Culture 2005, John was invited to sing a new composition 'Farranree', written especially for the occasion, at the official launch party – to a live audience of 100,000 people!

John collaborated with producer John Reynolds for his third album *Hey Dreamer,* which soared to No. 4 in the Irish album charts on the week of its release.

*Marc Roberts*

## Four Empty Walls

*Written by Marc Roberts*

*Taken from the album* Meet Me Half Way

Every weekend without fail, we used to visit my grandparents – my mum's parents. I remember as a kid, the long summer days helping out on the farm, then meeting all the extended family on Sundays in the house. In the space of a couple of years, both my grandparents passed away, and it was too difficult for any of us to go back to visit the house. So, one afternoon, without telling anyone, I decided to venture back to the farm. The wall around the house, which I remembered as a kid not being able to see over, I could now step over. The fields that were once manicured and tended were now overgrown, and the house, which held so many pleasant memories, was in ruin. All that was left was four empty walls.

## Four Empty Walls

*There's a faded old picture that hangs on the wall,*
*Its frame is clouded with dust,*
*A sepia print of a lifetime spent,*
*Surrounded by true love and trust,*
*There's a dirty old curtain that filters the light,*
*And blinds a once familiar view,*
*And an old rocking chair sits lonely and bare,*
*Reminiscing the life it once knew.*

*Chorus*
*If the grandfather clock could turn back its hands,*
*And change these cobwebs to ribbons and bands,*
*The laughter the tears and the heartaches we still recall,*
*We had all the love that we needed,*
*In these four empty walls.*

*In the field there's a tree and around it we played,*
*Now it's just wasting away,*
*But I can still see the names we engraved,*
*Of the sweethearts we'd loved for a day,*
*Now the lock on the door is rusted with time,*
*It hides all the memories inside,*
*And though nobody cares the fact it's still there,*
*Will always bring tears to my eyes.*

## BIOGRAPHY

It's a long way from the school hall in Crossmolina singing Don McLean's 'American Pie' to representing his country on the international stage singing in the Eurovision Song Contest before 300 million television viewers, but that's the remarkable journey undertaken by Mayo man Marc Roberts, who came second in the song contest with 'Mysterious Woman' in 1997. Appearances on The *Late Late Show*, *Richard & Judy*, *Open House* and the *Kelly Show* followed and, since then, Marc has been establishing himself as a live performer and singer-songwriter. He also has his own Saturday afternoon radio show on Galway Bay FM.

Marc has enjoyed critical acclaim for his tribute concert to the late John Denver, who is one of his influences along with other singer-songwriter legends like James Taylor, David Gates, Dan Fogelberg, Janis Ian and Carole King. He has also become a mentor to his showbiz pal Daniel O'Donnell, guiding and encouraging the superstar to become a songwriter. The fruit of this partnership has led to several O'Donnell/Roberts songs appearing on Daniel's recent top-selling albums.

Marc's songs are rich in emotional depth and bursting with heartfelt sentiment; they are songs of love and the politics of personal relationships. They trail through the trials and tribulations of life, offering hope and inspiration. Blessed with a creative mind, Marc has the added good fortune of possessing a honey combed voice, which is a perfect vehicle for his compositions.

There is a further Daniel O'Donnell connection on his album *Meet Me Half Way*. One of the album's stand-out tracks, 'When I Found You', was co-written by Marc and Daniel's then bride-to-be Majella as a surprise love song to her husband on their wedding day. Now, it's one of the most requested songs on Irish radio.

Marc has finally come of age as a songwriter with his third album *Once In Your Life*.

*Mick Flavin*

## The Old School Yard

*Written by Patsy Cavanagh*

*Taken from the album* Sweet Memory

I had the original idea for this song but I didn't actually write it – Patsy Cavanagh from Greencastle, County Donegal, wrote it for me. It was an idea that I had about the old school that I went to in Gaigue in Ballinamuck, County Longford, where I'm from. The school was closed and had been allowed to go wild and overgrown and the yard was full of potholes because someone had bought the land and was using part of the yard as a garage, but to look at the building from the road, it appeared that it had never been touched. There was a little river that flowed alongside it, and I incorporated all that into the song, 'The old schoolyard is wild and overgrown.'

When I was going to school, I used to cross the fields in the morning and hopped over a stile on the way. I bring that into the song as well, 'All the fences I have crossed have broken down and I've learned many things, some of them best forgotten since the first day that I stood upon that ground.' From deep inside, I see one of the children in the yard looking at the man that I turned out to be. It's kind of like I'm looking back to when I was a child and recalling all the happy days I spent in that yard, and a face is looking out at me and measuring up the kind of man I turned out to be.

'The Old School Yard' has a lot of emotion and precious memories for me. It is one of the most popular songs I have ever recorded and a song that would have really kick-started success for me.

The old school is still there, although it's been closed now for many years, but I did get into it one day to make a video to go with the song. There were two parts to it, Scoil na gCailíní on the left-hand side and Scoil na mBuachaillí on the right – even in those days there was segregation and the boys were separated from the girls!

### The Old School Yard

*I had walked down a road, a road full of memories,*
*On a journey back to visit childhood friends,*
*And I stopped at a gate that led into a schoolyard,*
*Long forgotten feelings come to me again.*

*The silence that stares from a dirty dusty window,*
*Broken only by the babble of a stream.*
*And I feel as though I am watched by a thousand different faces,*
*As I recollect a thousand different things.*

#### Chorus
*The old schoolyard is wild and overgrown,*
*All the fences I had crossed are broken down.*
*And I learned many things some of them best forgotten,*
*Since the last time I stood on that ground.*

*I close my eyes can't hold back the memories,*
*Childhood voices calling out to me.*
*From deep inside I see one of the faces looking,*
*At the man that he turned out to be.*

**Chorus**
*The old schoolyard is wild and overgrown*
*All the fences I had crossed are broken down*
*And I learned many things some of them best forgotten*
*Since the last time I stood on that ground*

## BIOGRAPHY

Mick Flavin grew up in a thatched farmhouse in the picturesque village of Ballinamuck, County Longford. Music played a big part in his childhood, and his cherished record player introduced him to the world of song and the delights of Buddy Holly, Eddie Cochran, Hank Williams and Tex Ritter.

He bought his first guitar as a youngster in Denniston's Music Shop in Longford for the princely sum of £4 and learned to play it from a guitar tutor. His natural talent was soon noticed and led to an offer to play in a local band when he was sixteen. For a number of years, he juggled his love of music with his trade as a carpenter, and moving to Dublin offered Mick a golden opportunity to see his favourite Country and Irish bands in action.

When he returned to Longford in the mid-1970s, Mick secured employment with Longford County Council and kept up his music on a part-time basis. In May 1978, the group he played with were invited to the USA for a month and, eight years later, another Longford man, Declan Nerney, encouraged Mick to record his first album. This he did, and the album was released in time for Christmas that same year.

The long-awaited sweet taste of success followed, and Mick went on to record with Harmac and Ritz Records, producing a total of twelve albums and three videos. He has been awarded with silver and gold discs and, in 2005, became the first Irish country artist to be nominated for the Country Music Association Global Artist Award.

*Patsy Watchorn*

## Dublin In The Rare Auld Times

*Written by Pete St John*

Although my favourite song of all would have to be 'The Isle Of Innisfree', I think for this book I'd have to pick 'Dublin In The Rare Auld Times'. It was written by Pete St John and was my biggest hit.

I first met Pete in the old Sheiling Hotel in Dublin back in 1975. He was after coming home from America and introduced himself as a songwriter and he had lots of songs. I was having a pint at the counter and looking through the songs when I spotted 'Rare Auld Times', and I thought it looked like a lovely song.

I used to sing it on stage when I played in the Embankment in Tallaght and Luke Kelly would say to me after I sang it, 'That's a beautiful song, you'll have to record it before someone else does.' So, in 1977, I recorded it in the old Eamonn Andrews Studio in Harcourt, Street and it took off. Then I went to America for four or five weeks, and when I came back, it had got into the charts, but it didn't get to No. 1 straight away. Then Danny Doyle brought it out and it went to the top.

I re-released it a while later, and it went to No. 1. Then, twenty-five years later, I rereleased it again and I got a gold album for it – first in 1977 and then another gold album twenty-five years later – and a week after that, it went platinum again!

## Dublin In The Rare Auld Times

*Raised on songs and stories, heroes of renown,*
*The passing tales and glories, that once was Dublin town,*
*The hallowed halls and houses, the haunting children's rhymes,*
*That once was part of Dublin, in the rare ould times.*

**Chorus**
*Ring-a-ring a-Rosie, as the light declines,*
*I remember Dublin City in the rare auld times.*

*My name it is Sean Dempsey, as Dublin as could be*
*Born hard and late in Pimlico in a house that ceased to be.*
*By trade I was a cooper, lost out to redundancy*
*Like my house that fell to progress, my trade's a memory.*

*And I courted Peggy Duignan, as pretty as you please,*
*A rogue and a Child of Mary, from the rebel Liberties,*
*I lost her to a student chap, with skin as black as coal,*
*When he took her off to Birmingham, she took away my soul.*

**Chorus**
*Ring-a-ring a-Rosie, as the light declines,*
*I remember Dublin city in the rare auld times.*

*Well the years have made me bitter, sure the gargle dimmed my brain,*
*'Cause Dublin keeps on changing and nothing seems the same.*
*The Pillar and the Met have gone, the Royal long since pulled down,*
*As the grey unyielding concrete makes a city of my town.*

**Chorus**
*Ring-a-ring a-Rosie, as the light declines,*
*I remember Dublin city in the rare auld times.*

*So fare thee well sweet Anna Liffey, I can no longer stay,*
*And watch the new glass cages that spring up along the Quay,*
*My mind's too full of memories, to listen to new chimes,*
*I'm a part of what was Dublin, in the rare auld times.*

**Chorus**
*Ring-a-ring a-Rosie, as the light declines,*
*I remember Dublin city in the rare auld times.*

## BIOGRAPHY

Patsy Watchorn was born into a very musical family. His father Ernest and his uncles all played piano, banjo, mandolin and fiddle, while his mother Christina was a singer. Music was a part and parcel of family life.

In the late 1960s, he sang and played with The Quare Fellas, and they recorded two albums before he left the group to pursue new directions.

The early 1970s saw him team up with Mick Crotty to form a new group and, along with two more recruits, The Dublin City Ramblers was born. As lead singer, Patsy's unique voice took him and his band to new heights. They toured all over Ireland and further afield, playing many of the prestigious Irish festivals in the USA and worldwide.

Album followed album, and hit followed hit, with many of Ireland's best-known songwriters penning songs for Patsy. Pete St John wrote 'Dublin In The Rare Auld Times', Liam Reilly of Bagatelle wrote 'Flight Of Earls' and Johnny McEvoy wrote ballads for him. Patsy collected gold, platinum and multi-platinum awards over the years and looks back at these years with pride.

By the mid-1990s, Patsy opted to change tack again and left the Ramblers to pursue a solo career. He subsequently released a compilation album, *The Very Best of Patsy Watchorn,* which went gold through sales in Dublin alone. His live schedule is as busy as ever, and he recently joined The Dubliners touring around Austria, Holland, Germany and Scotland.

Over the years, Patsy has recorded twenty-eight albums and has matured as one of Ireland's most recognisable ballad singers.

*Hearts On Fire,* released in 2003, includes such favourites as 'Dublin In My Tears', 'John O' Dreams', 'Step It Out Mary', 'Grace', 'Raglan Road', 'Galway To Graceland' and 'Ann Devlin', while *Irish Rebel Heroes,* released in 2004, includes the tracks 'God Save Ireland', 'Rising Of The Moon', 'Dublin In The Green', 'Upton Ambush', 'James Connolly', 'The Ballad Of Billy Reid' and 'Boys Of The Old Brigade'.

*Leo Moran — The Saw Doctors*

## Stars Over Cloughanover

*Written by Leo Moran and Davy Carton*

*Taken from the album* The Cure

We were in the process of recording our album *The Cure* in spring 2005 in Cuan Studios on the shores of Galway Bay in Spiddal. I'd leave Tuam at around 9.30 a.m. and drive to Davy's house in Claregalway to pick him up and we'd head for Spiddal, usually taking the back road by Moycullen where, from the crest of the hill on the twisty, bumpy back road, we could avail of the amazingly inspirational first view of the Atlantic. Even on a foggy or drizzly morning when we could see no ocean, no Aran Islands, nor Clare and the Burren across the bay, we still loved it.

This one morning, I left Tuam and was listening to Marian Finucane's chat show on RTÉ Radio One. She had an astronomer as a guest, whose name I didn't get, but I liked him from the start – he was able to make some of the mysteries of the universe sound comprehensible to the likes of me, and it was a pleasure listening to him. He stated that it was believed that in about 15 million years' time, some kind of giant meteorite would hit the earth and destroy it. Marian expressed a certain amount of shock, but he assured her that if the human race was still around at that stage it should have learned how to get to and inhabit other planets and, he added, so as to stop Marian worrying, 'It's a long time away yet.'

I picked Davy up in the car, and I have no idea what we recorded that day, but, after I left him back home in the evening, I drove to Headford to my girlfriend Eleanor's house. She lives a nice little walk away from a very interesting and entertaining pub a mile outside of the town heading towards Galway City. The pub is called Campbell's Tavern and is renowned for top-class music, hospitality and devilment. I walked over to the Tavern for a pint, the long evenings were asserting their presence, and the twilight journey on foot was a pleasure, filling my lungs with the green-tinged aromas, exclusive to the onset of the summertime.

Mick Bewick is a great friend and a great fisherman. He is an Englishman who loves and appreciates the great things about Ireland more than most of the natives. Mick nearly always catches fish on his beloved Corrib but, when he doesn't, he regards the mountains and relishes the lunch and the tea from the Kelly kettle on one of the islands. He equally enjoys the few pints and a few good songs afterwards in the pub. Mick was in the Tavern.

So was Don Stiffe, his fishing buddy, a native of Bohermore in Galway City, now married and living a stone's throw from the shores of Kenny's Bay. Don is also a talented angler. Not only that, but he possesses an extra-ordinarily strong and passionate voice, and when he sings the room falls silent because people know that they are hearing something special. Don was in the Tavern.

Up until recently, the house beside the Tavern was owned by Paddy Coyne, a native of Joyce country. Paddy plays the button accordion, and the tunes he plays, and the style with which he plays them, carry the ancient music of Connemara's ancestors into the twenty-first century. Paddy wasn't in the Tavern, but his son Pat was. Pat, or Pateen as he is affectionately known, and Don are musically very similar, though with styles uniquely their own. They both have exceptionally rich voices; they both have unusual and tasty reper-toires with songs off the beaten track. Songs you don't hear often and some songs you will have never heard before. And they both have a crafty mastery of backing themselves with the acoustic guitar, more often than not with unorthodox and interesting tunings.

Then there was Noelie McDonnell – originally from Tuam, now living locally – a man with a large number of top-class songs, who has since toured Britain as support act with The Saw Doctors and has put out his highly acclaimed debut album *Stars*. Noelie writes perceptively and evocatively as anyone who has heard his creations will testify.

Representing the local bikers and ex-drummers turned bass-players, guitarists and singers, was Will Merrigan. Will plays bass with Noelie and is well able to put over a good version of a blues song when the humour is on him – and it was.

Gert was there, a German by birth but living in Ireland for a good few years now. Gert plays great guitar, often with Noelie, and can make a fat-sounding electric guitar sing along with anyone. He sings songs in the sessions and introduces the bottleneck guitar to the sound every now and again.

Sandra Joyce came out from behind the bar and joined in, a woman with a rich voice and a collection of songs she'd be known for singing with The Lounge Lizards. We had a good team.

We talked fishing in the green room beside the dartboard, and Gert and Noelie and Will arrived with a couple of guitars. We drank soft, creamy pints of Guinness as the instruments were passed around, everyone giving a song in turn – Don, Mick, Gert, Pateen, Noelie, Will, Sandra and myself, and the circling of the guitar continued. It was magical, everyone was relaxed and in the mood, and everyone had the length of seven songs to decide what they'd sing next. Pateen asked Gert for the bottleneck and took to the slide acoustic guitar like he takes to everything musical – with the utmost of natural ease. It was a very special session, but it couldn't last forever, and sadly, but inevitably, it was time to walk home.

The night was clear the stars putting on a show of twinkling beauty and mystery. I looked up at them in the silent rural darkness, away from the lights of the towns and cities, and thought of 15 million years' time when Planet Earth would be no more and all its contents would be smashed out into space. For some reason, I thought about my hands – the cells, the bones, the blood, the skin – all separated by that time already, floating out there in vast, vast space. The line 'I will be part of you' came to mind as I gazed up at the heavenly bodies. I took out my mobile and recorded the line into the voice recorder.

Many times I've woken in the morning with one line recorded and not been able to remember back to what I was thinking of at the time, relieving me of any chance of using the idea for a song. For some reason, this went through my head, so, to remind me of what I was talking about in the morning, I recorded 'The Stars Over Cloughanover' into the phone and continued on my most enjoyable journey with the stars and the songs in my mind.

A few days later, I called to Davy, and we were sitting around in the kitchen drinking tea, and I remembered the couple of lines on my phone, so we started playing with the idea and, in no time at all, we had the song finished. It's very simple, probably couldn't be any simpler, but we liked it.

We almost didn't bring it to the sessions for the album as we had nearly finished most of the songs and may have had enough to finish the album. We were afraid that starting a new one at that stage might throw a spanner in the works, but we had a go at it, and it was easy, and it went down on tape in no time.

We have two guests on the recording of 'Stars Over Cloughanover'. Paul Barrett does the haunting backing vocal. Paul came out on the British tour the previous December with Noelie as the support act, and we were able to get him to Spiddal for an evening to try out a few things. Another Noelie connection was Nickie Geddes, a Scotswoman cellist living in Galway. She was a joy to work with, trying out ideas with the total absence of fuss. We'd always wanted to have a cello on some of our songs, and we couldn't have found a better person to work with.

So that's the 'Stars Over Cloughanover' – we will be part of them!

## Stars Over Cloughanover

*Late at night*
*I'm walking home*
*In the darkness*
*On my own*
*Breezes moving*
*Through the branches*
*Beside the castle*
*In the field*

*The stars are over*
*Cloughanover*
*I will be part of you*

*Scents of summer*
*Are all around me*
*I've left the talking behind*
*Walking slowly*
*I'm in no hurry*
*The night-time sky is mine*

*Some have gone now*
*To seek their fortune*
*In the lands*
*Beyond the seas*
*I'm still here now*
*In Cloughanover*
*Nowhere else*
*I'd rather be*

# BIOGRAPHY

To fully understand the intricate factors that led to the birth of Tuam's famous sons, we meet the town's very first punk band – BlazeX, of which Davy Carton was a member. Following their break-up in the mid-1980s, there remained 'a rake of songs left over', says Saw Doctors' Leo Moran who befriended Davy before recruiting John 'Turps' Burke and Padraig Stevens. Together, the fearless foursome began to play to audiences far and wide and went on to record Davy's composition 'All I Ever Wanted' in the salubrious surroundings of Tony Maher's studio in Renmore.

Padraig later returned to London, and the lads found a new drummer in Fergal 'Red' McGrath. They then recorded 'Dream Girl' and 'Summer Girl' (written by Padraig Stevens) in Kenny Ralph's studio, Tuam.

They then met with Derek Murray, guitar player, soundman and member of The Stunning, who assisted the Docs in recording 'Red Cortina' and, later, the infamous 'I Useta Lover'.

Mike Scott of The Waterboys asked them to support The Waterboys' Irish tour, so a new bass player was needed and they found him in Pearse Doherty. The tour led to a meeting with Phil Tennant, who was recording some concerts for The Waterboys; Phil went on to produce two of their albums, *If This Is Rock 'n' Roll, I Want My Old Job Back* and *All the Way from Tuam*.

A modest bank loan led to the recording of the 'N17', closely followed by 'It Won't Be Tonight', 'I Useta Love Her' and 'Sing A Powerful Song'. This was the turning point: 'I Useta Love Her' rose to No. 1, where it stayed for nine weeks. The band re-released 'N17' which then went to No. 2 in the Irish charts. Suddenly, The Saw Doctors were a household name and were even given the Freedom of Tuam! In 1991, they won an Irish Record Music Association (IRMA) award and, around the same time, embarked on their first solo tour of England. The first album *If This Is Rock 'n' Roll, I Want My Old Job Back* was released in 1991 and entered the Irish charts at No. 1. In September of the same year, the group played The West's Awake gig in Tuam with Mike Scott, The Hothouse Flowers and The Stunning.

In October 1991, The Saw Doctors embarked on their first US tour and, in 1992, *All The Way from Tuam* was released. February 1993 saw the release of 'Wake Up Sleeping', while 1994 was an extremely busy year for the band with a series of 'World Cup' concerts in America. In between their hectic touring schedule, The Saw Doctors set up their own independent label, Shamtown Records, in autumn 1994 and continued working on their third album. The first single on their own label, 'A Small Bit of Love' reached No. 24 in the UK charts and led to the Doc's first *Top of the Pops* appearance.

In 1996, they released a new single, 'World Of Good', which reached No. 15 in the UK, leading to the band's second *Top of the Pops* appearance. They also enjoyed another thirty-day, sell-out tour of England, Scotland and Wales, ending up with a brilliant gig in the Royal Court in Liverpool on St Patrick's Night. The album, *Same Old Town* was also released in this year, reaching No. 6 in the UK, receiving silver-disc status.

Their albums include *Live in Galway, Play It Again Sham, Villains, Sing a Powerful Song, Songs from Sun Street, Same Oul Town, All the Way From Tuam, If This Is Rock 'n' Roll, I Want My Old Job Back, Blaze X, Sound, New Year's Day* and *The Cure.*

*Brendan Bowyer*

## The Hucklebuck

*Written by Andy Gibson and Roy Alfred*

*Taken from the album* The Best of Brendan Bowyer

It's now nearly fifty years since the Royal Showband started in September 1957 at the Olympia Ballroom, Waterford, when seven teenagers began their journey to becoming Ireland's most popular showband.

'The Hucklebuck' is a song that has an amazing history. I didn't write it, although I did write a follow-up song called 'Hucklebuck Time Again'. But 'The Hucklebuck' was my most successful recording ever – recorded in 1964. It actually went platinum in world sales by the mid-1980s.

It was, however, jazz musician Paul Williams who first recorded this as an instrumental in 1948 and who then went on to feature his version of 'The Hucklebuck' at the now famous Moondog Ball, a show in the Cleveland Arena (now home of the Rock 'n' Roll Hall of Fame) on 21 March 1952. This was promoted by disc jockey Alan Freed and often called the first rock concert. Many vocal recordings were to follow, notably by Chubby Checker, but a swing version by Frank Sinatra was probably, indirectly, the reason I took to it. When I heard Ireland's most popular band at the time The Clipper Carlton featuring it as a swing-dance number, I learned it *rock style* and included it in our programme with the Royal Showband in 1962, so we were actually performing 'The Hucklebuck' on stage for two years before recording it in Abbey Road in 1964.

Because of our familiarity with the song, we managed to give it the infectious party atmosphere that made it such a big hit – the biggest ever in Ireland to that point – and a standard at discos, dances, even weddings, ever since. It proves a song doesn't have to be difficult to be great. I love singing it and feel privileged to be part of 'Hucklebuck' history.

## The Hucklebuck

*Here's a dance you should know*
*When the lights are down low*
*Grab your baby then go.*
*Do the Hucklebuck,*
*Do the Hucklebuck,*
*If you don't know how to do it*
*Boy you're out of luck!*
*Push your partner out*
*Then you hunch your back*
*Start a little movement in your sacroiliac.*
*Wiggle like a snake*
*Waddle like a duck*
*That's the way you do it*
*When you do the Hucklebuck.*

# BIOGRAPHY

Born in County Waterford, Brendan Bowyer is synonymous with the magic of the showband era and first came into prominence in 1959 as lead singer with the famous Royal Showband from the city of his birth.

His recordings with the Royal included six No. 1 hits, the most successful being 'The Hucklebuck', which went platinum internationally. The 1960s were the golden era when the Royal Showband staked their claim as Ireland's most popular showband. In 1961, they were voted the No. 1 Modern Dance Band in the UK and made the movie *The One Nighters*, which received a Special Award at the Cork Film Festival in 1963.

The 1980s saw Brendan juggle performing in Las Vegas with sell-out summer seasons at Clontarf Castle in Dublin. One of the most treasured memories of the 1970s was undoubtedly when the King himself, Elvis Presley, came to see them perform. Elvis was so impressed with Brendan's performance of 'You Gave Me A Mountain' that he later recorded it himself, included it in his own programme and also featured it on his worldwide special: *Aloha From Hawaii*.

Brendan made a welcome return to the recording studio in the 1990s and recorded the appropriately titled The *Best of Brendan Bowyer*, which included all his hits, including 'The Hucklebuck'. The next release was *Going Home*, a diverse collection of old and new songs, which accentuated his versatile skills, followed by *Brendan Bowyer's Ireland*, a compilation of his favourite Irish ballads.

His long-awaited revival came in 2001 with the release of 'The New Century' and the subsequent release of the album *Follow On*, his own tribute to some of Ireland's best-known singer-songwriters.

He continues to tour and perform with an enviable zest for life and is now joined by his daughter Aisling.

*Declan Nerney*

# The Marquee In Drumlish

*Written by Declan Nerney and Henry McMahon*

*Taken from the album* Three Way Love Affair

My most well-known song would probably be 'The Marquee In Drumlish' which I co-wrote with Henry McMahon of Big Tom and the Mainliners.

I would hope that the songs I sing are songs that people can identify with. Country and western is just a general term that's put upon these types of songs, but they are about real people and their real-life stories. They are about how people are seen in their own locality.

John Joe Reilly was a well-known footballer in Cavan, and there was a great ballad written about him called 'The Gallant John Joe'. That was a song about someone who existed in every community in Ireland. There was a 'John Joe' in every parish and in every county. And he represented all of those people who gave everything for their sport. That song is about what wearing the jersey meant to these people. If you sing a song like that with passion, it's always received well, whether you sing it in Kerry or Donegal or Cavan.

'The Marquee In Drumlish' is a similar sort of song because it incorporates my own life as well, and it is told through my own eyes. There was actually a marquee in Drumlish, and it ran successfully for the best part of fifteen years. It was a popular event at the start of every summer, and the dances were organised by the Drumlish footballers and the parish. I remember being a young boy at the time and it was an exciting time; it was the dawn of a new era and had all the trappings and excitement that came with that.

The song talks about how big those nights were, so long ago, and how popular the showbands were at the time and the way they were perceived by the people. It was a very iconic time in Ireland in the entertainment industry because marquee dancing was the main entertainment at the time. That was, as the film says, 'as good as it gets'; and when this song came out, it brought people right back to that time of their lives. It became a chunk of history, and that's what I think makes a good song. If you can carve out a piece of history and land it on somebody's shoulder so much so that they are back there in that time and place, then you're doing something right.

I think the song became so successful because Henry McMahon was speaking from his place as a musician on the stage, and I was speaking from the dance floor and what it was like growing up at the time.

'The Marquee In Drumlish' became a proud song though it didn't set out to be, but a song takes on a personality of its own; there are some great songs written and you think that they will do well for you, but it might not happen that way. It's all about how a song is perceived and what personality that song takes on.

## The Marquee In Drumlish

*When I was just a little boy*
*My one and only wish*
*Was to get to see the showbands*
*Play the marquee in Drumlish*
*I'd watch them all arrive*
*In fine wagons and in cars*

*And I wondered what it would be like*
*To be a country star*

*My father used to tell me*
*That I was far too small*
*And I had no chance to go to the dance*
*To see the bands at all*
*But my mother would get round him*
*And I would get my wish*
*And we'd go to see the Mainliners*
*In the marquee in Drumlish*

*I'd watch Seamus McMahon*
*As he played his lead guitar*
*And I wondered how he got that sound*
*That's loved so near and far*
*When Big Tom sang 'Gentle Mother'*
*Sure I can tell you this*
*That everyone would sing along*
*In the marquee in Drumlish*

*Larry and the Mighty Avons*
*Were among my favourites too*
*How I envied Mickie Brady*
*With his fender colour blue*
*When Larry sang, 'He'll have to go'*
*Low notes he'd never miss*
*You could hear that Benson echo*
*Round the marquee in Drumlish*

*Philomena's country flavour*
*Would take the old bandstand*
*And I'd watch young Dan O'Hara*
*Pick and play 'My Ramblin Man'*

*And later on when I got home*
*I'd check the old jam jar*
*To see if I had saved enough*
*To buy my first guitar*

*So next morning with my mother*
*We went to Longford Town*
*And she bought me that first guitar*
*I think it cost twelve pounds*
*With radio and records*
*I'd practise all alone*
*Soon I had the job with The Hi-Lows*
*And Gene Stuart from Tyrone*

*And then one Friday evening*
*Came the biggest break of all*
*I was asked to join The Buckaroos*
*With the mighty Brian Coll*
*We played all over Ireland*
*England and the USA*
*And I owe a lot to Brian*
*For what I am today*

*And now the people tell me*
*That I could go far*
*We play all over Ireland*
*From Cork to Castlebar*
*The carnival is over*
*But I still got my wish*
*For I got my inspiration*
*In the marquee in Drumlish*
*No I won't forget the marquee*
*In my native town Drumlish*

# BIOGRAPHY

Declan was raised on a small farm in Drumlish, County Longford, with his brother Gerry and two sisters, Ann and Bridget. He was heavily influenced by the music of Joe Dolan, Big Tom, Philomena Begley and the Capital Showband, and as a youngster always dreamt of performing on stage like his heroes.

At sixteen years of age, he secured his chance to live that dream with an invitation to join the showband The Hi-Los who were based in the Roscommon/Longford region. There, he served his early musical apprenticeship before progressing to The Gene Stuart Band and then to Brian Coll and The Buckaroos before eventually, in the late 1980s, he made the decision to start his own band. He has toured extensively in Ireland, England, Scotland, and the USA. In 1990, he sang to 65,000 people in Croke Park at half time in the All-Ireland final between Meath and Cork, with thousands more watching on television.

As a solo artist, he has enjoyed great success with the 'Marquee In Drumlish', 'Anna From Fermanagh', 'Gotta Get Up In The Morning', 'Stop the World', 'Let Me Off' and 'Take This Job And Shove It', as well as numerous gold-selling albums, including *Walking on New Grass*, *Three Way Love Affair*, *Going Round and Round*, *Let's Dance*, *The One and Only* and his latest *I Want To Love Again* which includes the self-penned track 'Barry And Dunne'.

Declan also came up with the novel idea of an annual Hooley in the Sun where he, as the name suggests, offers his most loyal fans the opportunity to travel to a sun-filled destination and see him join the crème de la crème of Irish artists in a party to rival all parties. In its third year, the Hooley in the Sun brought 350 revellers to the Spanish resort of Fuengirola, while organisers decided on Lanzarote for the 2006 event. Amongst those on the billing are Larry Cunningham, Susan McCann, Brian Coll, Hugo Duncan, TR Dallas, PJ Murrihy and Seamus Shannon.

Clearly proud of his roots, Declan is currently in the process of building a top-of-the-range luxury hotel in his native Drumlish. The new establishment will be called after his father, who was affectionately known as Dan Joe.

Declan has recently celebrated the release of his album *I Want to Love Again* and continues his mammoth success in the Irish country scene.

*Tony Allen — Foster and Allen*

## Bunch Of Thyme

*Old English folk song*

*Taken from the album* Foster and Allen's Ireland

One of my favourite songs would be 'Bunch Of Thyme'. It's an old English folk song and it has been very good to us. Foster and Allen started out in 1975; in 1976, we released an album, and, a year later, we were making another one and we were choosing songs for it. Myself and Mick were doing the cabaret circuit at the time, and I remember hearing Christy Moore singing 'Bunch Of Thyme', but people didn't listen to it much because, in those days, they were dancing to old-time waltzes and 'Bunch Of Thyme' was very slow.

Donie Cassidy was in my house one night, and it was snowing hard. Himself and his wife got up to go and, when I saw the snow, I told them to come back in and have a cup of tea and wait for it to stop. Then I just thought of the Christy Moore album and took it down and played it, and Donie said, 'Yes, that's a lovely song. You should record it for an album track.' When the album was finished, our producer Liam Hurley rang Donie and said, 'I can't get this song "Bunch Of Thyme" out of my head, it keeps haunting me.' So Donie said he'd listen to it, and Liam convinced our record company to bring it out as a single. It went to No. 1 in the Irish charts and we put 'The Blacksmith' on the B-side. The single has been in the Irish charts five or six times over the years and has been No. 1 twice.

Then Donie took 'Bunch Of Thyme' to England. He went over and approached every record label in England, and, at one stage, got it signed up with one but nothing happened. Then Ritz Records, which was run by Mick Durcan, an Irishman living in England, approached Donie for 'Bunch Of Thyme', and Donie actually had to remortgage his house and buy back the track! It was then released on the Ritz label.

In March 1982, it was No. 18 in the Irish charts. We were in the UK on tour and Donie rang us and said, 'Lads, you'd better get home because this record is in the Top 20, and if it's in the Top 20 next week you'll be on *Top of the Pops*!' We arrived home on a Tuesday morning in Dublin and sat in Donie's office until 12.00 p.m. when the news came through that it had got into the Top 20 in England. Donie had a flight booked – we flew to London on the Tuesday night, we recorded the show on Wednesday and it came out on *Top of the Pops* on Thursday. Then, of course, it went back into the Irish charts, and 'Bunch Of Thyme' started the ball rolling for Foster and Allen.

In one of his books, Christy Moore said that little did he know when he brought 'Bunch Of Thyme' back from England that it was going to launch Foster and Allen!

### Bunch Of Thyme

*Come all ye maidens young and fair*
*And you that are blooming in your prime*
*Always beware and keep your garden fair*
*Let no man steal away your thyme*

**Chorus**

*For thyme it is a precious thing*
*And thyme brings all things to my mind*
*Thyme with all its flavours, along with all its joys*
*Thyme, brings all things to my mind*

*Once I had a bunch of thyme*
*I thought it never would decay*
*Then came a lusty sailor*
*Who chanced to pass my way*
*And stole my bunch of thyme away*

**Chorus**

*For thyme it is a precious thing*
*And thyme brings all things to my mind*
*Thyme with all its flavours, along with all its joys*
*Thyme, brings all things to my mind*

*The sailor gave to me a rose*
*A rose that never would decay*
*He gave it to me to keep me reminded*
*Of when he stole my thyme away*

**Chorus**

*For thyme it is a precious thing*
*And thyme brings all things to my mind*
*Thyme with all its flavours, along with all its joys*
*Thyme, brings all things to my mind*

# BIOGRAPHY

Mick Foster and Tony Allen first teamed up together to play in local groups in the Midlands back in 1975. They soon spread their wings and started playing the Irish music venues in the UK with a small band. When the tour was over, Mick and Tony saw the band return home, while they concentrated their musical efforts as a duo, combining easy-listening music with a touch of traditional Irish instrumentation. So favourable was the response that they decided to remain together, and Foster and Allen was formed.

Having toured and performed solidly in both Ireland and the UK for a number of years, they released their first single 'The Rambles Of Spring', but it was their follow-up release 'Bunch of Thyme', that really moved things on to an altogether new and higher level.

The run of hit singles continued, including 'Maggie', 'I Will Love You All My Life' and 'After All These Years', and their careers took on a truly international dimension with high-profile concert tours in Canada, South Africa, the USA, Australia and New Zealand. 'Maggie' spent five weeks at No. 1 in Australia alone.

Foster and Allen have made numerous television appearances across the globe and have released more than thirty albums to date, all of which have been in the UK and Irish charts and the vast majority of which have achieved gold status in the UK.

Their latest album, *Foster & Allen Sing the No. 1s,* was also in the Top 30 in the UK, and *The Guinness Book of Records* lists them as the only act to have had an album in the British charts every year solidly from 1984 to 1999.

Foster and Allen have come a long way in the past thirty years, but their unique style and easy-listening sound remains as fresh and exciting as ever. Mick and Tony, along with their concert band, have delighted audiences in every corner of the globe with their own very special brand of music and humour.

*Christie Hennessy*

## Mr Blue

*Written by Christie Hennessy*

*Taken from the album* Lord of Your Eyes

I've picked a song called 'Mr Blue'. I wrote it after I heard a very moving story on the radio one night. I didn't get the full gist of what the man was saying but it seemed to be a very interesting story, and, over the next few days, I started thinking about it and wrote this song.

The story goes that there was this man who lived in New York and he was a big businessman. Every day, he was collected to go to work in a chauffeur-driven car. On one of the days, he said, 'I think I'll be like everyone else and take the train,' which was something he hadn't done in years. He didn't go where he wanted to go, he got on the wrong train and was shocked when he came to this remote village. He sat there and asked himself, 'What the Hell am I doing here? I'm miles away from where I should be.' He got off the train and started to walk around the station and have a look around, still not knowing why he was there, and he was actually late for work by now.

Standing on the corner was a dishevelled little girl. He looked at her and she was really out of place. She was wearing a dress that was too big for her and shoes that were too big for her. He went over to her and said, 'Are you waiting for somebody?' and she said, 'Yes' and he asked, 'Who?' and she said, 'I don't know.' It turned out that he'd been there ten years earlier and had met a woman. This little girl had been coming back to the station for nine hours every day when she should have been at school and she had no idea why ... It turned out that the little girl was actually his daughter!

It was an amazing story, and there was a book published on it later. The man was unaware that he had a daughter, but he knew there was a reason why he went to that station. I missed a large part of the story and it aggravated me for a long time. My wife even wrote to the radio station and asked them to repeat the story, and they said they would but they didn't. I felt I had to write something about it, and I wrote 'Mr Blue'. Now I sing the song with my own daughter.

### Mr Blue

*On my way through*
*I met Mr Blue*
*My friend the rain was cooling me down*
*If only I'd phoned*
*I might have known*
*Not to get off at this one-horse town*

*So unaware*
*Why I was standing there*
*I used to ride a fast train*
*But I was going nowhere*
*Looking around*
*Feeling like a clown*
*That I knew*
*When I saw you there*

*I felt that I should care*
*You wore a red dress*
*Your bigger sister should wear*
*But when you smiled*
*You looked just like a child*
*That I knew*

*'Hey Mr Blue*
*Say how do you do?*
*I have been waiting here for years*
*I always knew*
*You would come through*
*If you've got time*
*I'll show you around'*

*While you've been here*
*I've been everywhere*
*Walking backwards*
*Looking for a soft chair*
*Have I got time?*
*The rest of my life*

*Oh Mr Blue*
*What shall we do?*
*I guess that I should say, 'I love you' (x3)*

## BIOGRAPHY

A native of Tralee, County Kerry, Christie's strong accent has never faltered, despite more than forty years in the UK where he is now based.

With one of his daughters, Hermonie, singing and playing the piano, his son Timmy on keyboard and saxophone and another daughter, Amber excelling on the violin, it's clear that it's a musical love affair that has spanned generations.

Both his father and his mother had a profound influence on him musically when he was growing up, with his father playing the accordion and his mother, singing and telling stories.

Generally regarded as one of Ireland's most prolific singer-songwriters, having notched up five triple-platinum albums, Christie has also produced, written and performed with a wide range of recording stars, including Jools Holland, Mary Black, Yazz, Aled Jones, Beverley Craven and Tanita Tikaram, while Frances Black, Eleanor Shanley, Máire Brennan, Christy Moore and Foster and Allen have all enjoyed great success with his songs.

Having made his name as a songwriter, Christie Hennessy's instant rapport with an audience draws sell-out crowds to his live gigs. Amongst his many gems are 'If You Were To Fall', 'Lonely Boy', 'She's A Lovely Girl', 'I'm Going To Make It On My Own', 'Oh Jealous Heart', 'Believe In Me', 'Angel', 'All The Lies That You Told Me', 'Roll Back The Clouds', 'Messenger Boy', 'Remember Me' and 'Glory, Glory'.

*Christie Hennessy: The Platinum Collection,* was released late 2006.

# The Loneliness of Loss

*Christy Moore*

## The Two Conneeleys

*Written by Christy Moore*

*Taken from the album* King Puck

I was on holidays on the beautiful island of Inishmaan. One morning, as I walked out early, the atmosphere had totally changed. I saw an elderly lady lean against a stone wall steadying herself as she viewed the sea through binoculars. There seemed to be a lot of activity on the ocean. The birds had stopped singing. Later, at breakfast, we heard that two fishermen were missing out of Inisheer. I wrote this song to mark their passing.

### The Two Conneeleys

*Hear the Atlantic seethe and swell,*
*hear the lonesome chapel bell,*
*God save their souls and mind them well,*
*the two fishermen Conneeleys.*

*Yesterday at half past four*
*they pushed their currach from the shore,*
*one took the net and one took the oar,*
*the two fishermen Conneeleys.*

*From Connors Fort and from Synge's chair,*
*towards Inishmore and Inisheer,*
*they scour the sea in silent prayer,*
*as they go searching for their neighbours.*

*Día Dhíobh a bheirt iascairí brea,*
*nach mbeidh ar ais ar bharr an trá.*
*Go mbeidh dhíobh sonas sásta ar neamh,*
*Tomás agus Seán Ó Coinnghíle.*

*Draw the seaweed up the hill,*
*sow potatoes in the drill,*
*try to understand God's will*
*and the loss of the two Conneeleys.*

*Hear the Atlantic seethe and swell,*
*hear the lonesome chapel bell,*
*God save their souls and mind them well,*
*Tomás agus Seán Ó Coinnghíle.*

## BIOGRAPHY

Christy Moore was born in 1945 in Moorefield, Newbridge, County Kildare. He sang from early boyhood and made his first public appearance as a boy soprano in the Palace Cinema where he sang 'Kevin Barry' and 'The Meeting of the Waters'.

In 1966, Christy decided to take a chance and moved to England where he secured work on buildings, factories and oil rigs – yet he retained a hunger to perform and ended up on the folk-club circuit in Manchester in 1967.

Recognition was just around the corner, and, in 1968, Christy did his first radio broadcast on Dublin's O'Connell Street, during which he sang 'The Galtee Mountain Boy' and 'Bogie's Bonnie Belle'. In 1969, he auditioned unsuccessfully for Transatlantic and, subsequently, went on to record his first album *Paddy on the Road* with Dominic Behan at Sound Techniques in Chelsea, London.

Having failed his Transatlantic audition, Christy returned to producer Bill Leader who had begun releasing albums on his two record labels, Trailer and Leader. In July 1970, Bill arrived in Prosperous, County Kildare, where Christy had been rehearsing with Dónal Lunny, Andy Irvine and Liam O'Flynn. There they recorded material released as *Prosperous*. The four reconverged to form a band that began to play on Monday, 3 January 1972 with a residency upstairs in Slattery's on Dublin's Capel Street. They briefly called themselves CLAD but then settled on Planxty.

The first Planxty tour began at the MSG Manchester on 22 April 1972. Over the next two years, the band continued to tour and developed a loyal following. They recorded three albums *Planxty*, *The Well Below the Valley* and *Cold Blow and the Rainy Night*. Dónal left in 1974, and Christy left in 1975 to pursue his dreams alone again.

In 1978, Planxty reformed and began to rehearse for the *After the Break* album. The original four members were joined by Matt Molloy. In January 1979, they began to rehearse for their longest tour, which began in The Hammersmith Odeon, London, on Saturday, 15 April and finished in The Stadium, Dublin, on Monday, 11 June, with the band performing fifty-four concerts in eight countries.

By 1982, Christy was playing with Moving Hearts and Planxty as well as doing solo gigs.

The 1990s saw the recording of *Smoke and Strong Whiskey* and *King Puck*, and, by 2000, Christy had branched into writing and had published his auto-biography, *One Voice*.

Christy's most popular albums include *King Puck*, *Ride On*, *Ordinary Man*, *Voyage* and *Burning Times*, which is dedicated to the memory of the American peace activist Rachel Corrie, who lost her life in Gaza. Christy's most recent album is *Christy Moore, Live at the Point, 2006*.

*Eric Bogle*

## Leaving Nancy

*Written by Eric Bogle*

*Taken from the album* Now I'm Easy

Asking me which song that I have composed means the most to me is a difficult question. The answer is of course, *all* of them, they all mean a great deal to me in their individual ways. But if I'm forced to make a choice, then I nominate 'Leaving Nancy'. This is a song I wrote for my mother Nancy when I left Scotland in 1969 to emigrate to Australia. It was, in fact, the first song I wrote in Australia, and in the song I say some things that I didn't have the courage or wit to say at the actual parting. It was a very painful goodbye, not so much for the emotions expressed at the time, but for all the emotions that were suppressed and all the things that were left unsaid. It was, in many ways, a typical Scots working-class parting. We talked about everything except the fact that I was going to the other end of the world and that we might never see each other again; we just made inconsequential small talk. All very polite, controlled, almost jovial, but the fierce, almost painful grip of

Nancy's hand on mine left me in no doubt about the depths of her true feelings. When the train started to pull away from the platform, and I leaned out of the window to wave goodbye, she started to cry, and the last sight I had of her was standing on the platform with tears streaming down her face. It was a long, long trip to Southampton …

Nancy died in 1975, but she got to hear 'her' song before she went. I sent her a tape of it from Australia shortly after I wrote it. It was her favourite song, of course, and so it became one of mine. She loved it, and I loved her, how then could it not be? I make no great claims for the song, either lyrically or melodically. Some people find it overly sentimental, but I don't care all that much what other people think of it. I think one of the reasons I like singing it is that, when I do sing it, Nancy lives again for the three-and-a-half minutes or so that the song lasts – for me at least. It's one of the great gifts that a songwriter has: he or she can bring past ghosts to life again in their songs, however briefly. It's like a small form of immortality I suppose.

It's a deeply personal song, but every human being on this planet knows only too well the pain of leaving loved ones, so it's been recorded quite a few times by various artists, the most notable version being by The Fureys. But who really cares how many people have recorded it? That wasn't the reason the song was written in the first place. I recorded 'Leaving Nancy' on my very first recording, an LP I made back in 1974 called *Now I'm Easy*. I subsequently featured a 'live' version on a compilation CD, *Eric Bogle: By Request,* which I released in 1996.

## Leaving Nancy

*In comes the train and the whole platform shakes*
*Stops with a shutter and a screaming of brakes*
*The parting has come and my weary soul aches*
*I'm leaving my Nancy-o*

*You stand there so calmly, determinedly gay*
*You talk of the weather and events of the day*
*And your eyes tell me all that your tongue doesn't say*
*Goodbye, my Nancy-o*

**Chorus**
*And come a little closer*
*Put your head upon my shoulder*
*And let me hold you one last time*
*Before the whistle blows*

*My suitcase is lifted up and stowed on the train*
*And a thousand regrets whirl around in my brain*
*The ache in my heart is a black sea of pain*
*I'm leaving my Nancy-o*

*But you stand there beside me, so lovely to see*
*The grip of your hand is a non-spoken plea*
*You're a-fooling yourself, but you're not fooling me*
*Goodbye, my Nancy-o*

**Chorus**
*And come a little closer*
*Put your head upon my shoulder*
*And let me hold you one last time*
*Before the whistle blows*

*But our time has run out and the whistle has blown*
*Here I must leave you standing alone*
*We'd so little time and now the time's gone*
*Goodbye, my Nancy-o*

*And as the train starts gently to roll*
*And as I lean out to wave and to call*
*I see the first tears trickle and fall*
*Goodbye, my Nancy-o*

**Chorus**
*And come a little closer*
*Put your head upon my shoulder*
*And let me hold you one last time*
*Before the whistle blows*

*And let me hold you one last time*
*Before the whistle blows*

## BIOGRAPHY

Eric is the son of a bagpipe player from Peebles in Scotland. He wrote poetry from early childhood and, raised on a diet of Elvis Presley and Lonnie Donegan, he taught himself to play the guitar and joined a series of rock bands. He left school at sixteen and undertook a variety of jobs, including manual labourer, export clerk and bartender.

Eric emigrated to Australia in 1969 and worked as an accountant, but music was never far from his mind, and he became involved with a folk club in Canberra. It was 'And The Band Played Waltzing Matilda' that first brought him international prominence, followed by the haunting 'No Man's Land' ('Green Fields of France'). The Furey's rendition of this song stayed in the Irish music charts for a staggering twenty-six weeks.

His released material includes 'Now I'm Easy', 'Plain And Simple', 'Scraps Of Paper', 'Singing The Spirit Home', 'Something Of Value', 'When The Wind Blows', 'Hard, Hard Times', 'Voices In The Wilderness', 'The Emigrant And The Exile', 'Small Miracles', 'Mirror', 'Endangered Species', 'The Colour Of Dreams' and 'Other People's Children'. He is currently working on his fifteenth release.

Throughout his lengthy career, his songs have been recorded by many artists, including The Pogues, Mary Black, Joan Baez and Donovan.

During 2006, Eric and his band-mates, John Munro, Ian Blake, Brent Miller, Dave O'Neill, Jon Jones and Andy McCloin, toured throughout Ireland, the UK, Scotland, Alaska, the USA, Denmark and Australia.

Over the past couple of decades, Eric Bogle has appeared in many music festivals around the world and has been the recipient of many awards for his music, including a UN Peace Medal and The Order of Australia from the Australian Government.

*Maria Butterly*

## Kieran

*Written by Maria Butterly*

*Taken from the album* It's Just Me

I was just seventeen years old, about to turn eighteen, and was in a band from Balbriggan and hung out with a group of friends in Stamullen, Gormanston, County Meath. It was St Stephen's night, and we all met in a pub called The Hen. Across the main Dublin–Belfast road was another pub called The Cock. At 9.20 p.m., Kieran showed up in great form sporting a new sweater that his sister had given him as a Christmas present.

Kieran was twenty-one – the kindest, most endearing, good lad that a mam and dad could wish to have for a son. He was the second youngest, with an older brother, a younger brother and a sister. He would occasionally come to gigs and help us out with the lights. He was kind-hearted and would do anything for you. There was no drama, he just went with the flow. Everyone loved Kieran, he was a real gentleman. He'd give you the shirt off his back.

I had the privilege of hanging around with a good group from Stamullen. We were all into music and bands, some of the lads were real headrockers. We were all just trying to get up and running with our lives. Sometimes being in Stamullen was a blessing and a nice break from my own problems at home.

We had been joking a bit – as I remember, Kieran's new jumper was blue and white, with a clouds-and-sheep pattern. He was also wearing tight jeans and white runners and was all set to go for his night out. He wasn't going out with us but had just stopped in The Hen on his way into town as he was meeting some friends, as were we. We were all heading into Drogheda to see a band called Winter's Reign. It was early enough as we had arrived in The Hen ourselves at 8.30 p.m.. Everyone was in good form, still sober and having fun. Then it was time for us to call for a taxi to meet up with our other friends who had gone ahead to keep seats for us for the band show. The phone in The Hen was not working, so Kieran went across the road to use the phone in The Cock. Time was getting on and we began to wonder where he was; then there was a lot of commotion outside and our fun, exciting night started to turn into the most horrific night of my life.

Kieran never made it back inside the pub to finish his first pint – only a sip of it was taken as it sat there by itself waiting on his return to finish and enjoy. He did make the call over in The Cock and the taxi was on its way, he made it back across the main Dublin–Belfast road, but there was a side road at the corner of the pub leading onto the main road – and this was what took our friend. A car came around the corner and skidded to avoid him, then the second car hit him, 30 feet up into the air. He was gone instantly.

When I ran out, I recognised him by his Christmas sweater. It was a night of turmoil. It was too intense to go into in detail. His own brother was one of the onlookers standing there, wondering who or what had happened; I had to turn away as I couldn't face being the one to tell him who it was.

And I kept running from that night – for almost fourteen years.

I live in LA now, and I wrote the song 'Kieran' almost five years ago. I went into the studio to record it, and I was having trouble getting the emotion of the story across. I tried many times in the studio, and then, upon driving home one night, I was thinking about how to sing it and what was really troubling me. I was so blocked in some areas of that night. I broke down, not with my car, but a pure breakdown of emotions and the truth of that night, which I had not admitted to myself or anyone else in fourteen years. I did not attend Kieran's funeral. I went to work on that day I was so terrified at being around his parents, who I didn't really know that well. I was just so afraid and full of anger and of what, I couldn't tell you at that time.

But I pulled over in my car and screamed out loud to Kieran above and God, if there was any, that I was sorry, that I was *so sorry*, and could he or anyone forgive me, *ever*? 'Why?' you ask? Well, the block was lifted, and I realised that I had personally asked Kieran that night, as we sat up on the bar stools, if he would go over to the other pub and call a taxi to come and get us.

As he left the bar stool, I almost got up to go with him as I was getting bored waiting for everyone to get ready to go, but I just sat back and said, 'He'll be back in a minute.' I felt so responsible, and from listening to others that night, they all felt somewhat responsible, not just me. Kieran's father said he gave him £20 that night to go out. My boyfriend's father felt responsible: he met Kieran as he headed down the 2 mile road to the pub. He picked him up and gave him a lift – he felt he gave him a lift to his final destination.

One of my other friends, I later learned, felt responsible, as she was sort of tipsy that night and was upset with something, which had urged me to ask Kieran to call for the taxi, to get into town before she got worse.

In December 2005, I came home to Ireland as my father was dying from prostate cancer. I called Kieran's house and spoke with his father (his mother had passed away five years previously). I told him who I was and that I had written a song about Kieran. I knew I would have to tell him, to some extent, what had happened that night. My mother came with me for support – eighteen years later I was still terrified and ashamed.

We got there and he welcomed me with open arms. He was just like Kieran, full of warmth, a soft, quiet man who had suffered a lot of losses in his life. I played the song from the CD for both Kieran's father and his brother. They were speechless and so touched that someone would actually still remember Kieran, that his life was not forgotten and that he had made an impact in the short time he was here. They were so happy, it was a very emotional day.

And then came the question. 'What actually happened that night?' his father asked. 'Nobody could really give me a straight answer and everyone disappeared after the funeral.' So I told him everything, and we both sobbed, and he took my hand like a father would to console the child, and said, 'You have done me a great healing. For fifteen years, I have not known exactly the full story of what happened to my son, and I just wanted an answer for the truth.'

During the trial of the person who hit Kieran, it was claimed that Kieran was most likely intoxicated, stumbling back across the road, but unfortunately no one came forth to stand up for him. He left his house at 9.00 p.m. and got his first pint, like I said, and took a sip from it and left to ring the taxi. It was still sitting there at 9.30 p.m., but all of us were too afraid to come forward – we were too young and afraid.

Imagine how I felt after hearing that. I wished I had had the courage back then and could have set things straight and cleared Kieran's name.

As you know at funerals, when you give a mass card, you get a memorial card sent to you with a picture of the person inside with a prayer. I lost mine, and, for years, I would go on a rampage looking for it. Maybe I had slipped it inside a book or something, but I never found it.

That day, before I left Kieran's house, his father came into the room and handed me the last card that he had and said, 'I thought you might like to have this.' Well the floodgates opened with tears of joy, and such a relief, like I have never experienced before, came over me! It was the start of Kieran's presence in my life and how this story has inspired and spiralled the amazing things that have happened.

I was at a party in LA one evening, and this couple were expecting their first child. I was performing at this party and sang 'Kieran'. I met the same couple at another party after they had their child; they called me over and said they had something to share with me. There in a rocking chair, was a little bundle all wrapped up. They had had a baby boy and had named their baby Kieran after hearing the song. This was more good news to relate back to Kieran's father.

Soon after, I was back home with my own father, who had never really heard me sing the kind of songs that he wanted me to sing. On Christmas Day, I got to sing one of the most beautiful festive songs, 'O Holy Night' at our local church. My father was in bed and my brother turned on the radio to tune into the Sunday mass services in our local church in Laytown, and the only time this radio station comes on is at mass times for the sick. My father got to hear me sing for his first and last time, the most beautiful song that he loved.

He was not a man for emotionally loving words, but he said, 'Ria, you're gonna be a millionaire,' and he had tears in his eyes as he said it.

I knew right then that my father really understood that my music career was really *real* for me, and not just a dream, but that I was living my dream, and he realised how good at it I was.

## Kieran

*I remember the happy days when we were so young*
*I remember our ways of doing things, oh boy were we dumb*
*Don't really see the guys or girls, I guess they're gone their own ways*
*Doing the best that I can, I'm doin' OK*

*I remember you puttin' up the lights for the band we were ready to play*
*A signal from your hand and the show was underway*
*Wild and wacked were our friends that came to see us play*
*How we thought the night would never end until came that fatal day*

### (Pre-chorus)
*I knew you had a heart of gold and the minute you were taken we were*
*undersold but that was your plan from a higher command*
*A signal from up above, you were on your way to another place*
*While we were left to face another day, Kieran*

### Chorus
*Every now and then I get a little glimpse of your smiling face*
*Bet your laughin' down at all our sweet mistakes*
*Every now and then I feel a warm embrace*
*Is it you tryna' catch the tears from my face*

*Unprepared for that car on that fatal day*
*You hit the ground with a force I knew you were gone*
*Sickened by these words be strong and carry on*
*This plan of action was so unfair, how could we carry on*

### (Pre-chorus)

*I knew you had a heart of gold and the minute you were taken we were*
*undersold but that was your plan from a higher command*
*A signal from up above, you were on your way to another place*
*All the good things how could this one do you so wrong*

### Chorus

*Every now and then I get a little glimpse of your smiling face*
*Bet you're laughin' down at all our sweet mistakes*
*Every now and then I feel a warm embrace*
*Is it you tryna' catch the tears from my face*

### Bridge

*I remember the days when we were young*
*Kieran, I hope all is well in your new place*
*Hold on, cause it won't be long till we see you*
*Kieran…*

### Instrumental

*Kieran, I hope all is well in your new place*
*Hold on, cause it won't be long till I see you*
*Kieran*

## BIOGRAPHY

County-Meath-born singer-songwriter Maria Butterly is a Celtic tour de force. Her original style of music opens the door to a Celtic country craze, and she lets loose with a raw-edged passion. Young Maria taught herself to play various instruments, including the guitar, viola, mandolin, whistles and piano. Her voice is a gift inherited from her mother and her lyrics are warm, positive and upbeat, ranging from love ballads to rants to the conquering of life's struggles.

After spending some time in New York, Maria travelled to Nashville where she had a chance to study her craft and was offered her first publishing deal for her song entitled 'Silent Partner'. Eventually, she made her way to Los Angeles, California, where she now lives.

Maria and her band have opened for Damien Rice, Michelle Shocked, The Proclaimers, The Hothouse Flowers, The Saw Doctors, The Fenians, Dolores Keane and Stockton's Wing.

She performed at the Angelica Huston Gala Event at the Beverly Hilton Hotel and has been the recipient of the Best Irish Folk Award in the New York International Film and Music Festival.

While on tour in New York, Maria met with three-time Grammy winner, mixing engineer Elliot Scheiner, at the famous Avatar Studios and sat in with Elliot on a mixing session for Donald Fagan from Steely Dan.

She has performed in many clubs, including House of Blues, The Roxy, The Troubadour (New York's oldest rock club), The Mercury Lounge, Nashville's Bluebird Café and Nine Fine Irishmen at the New York Hotel in Las Vegas. She also performs at theatre concert venues and large outdoor festivals and has played all around Ireland.

In 2005, she released an acoustic solo CD titled *It's Just Me,* which features seven tracks that she herself arranged, performed and produced.

Maria is very much a positive example of an independent artist making it in the world of music. She set up her own recording studio in Los Angeles and produced her latest album *The Turning Point,* released in 2006.

*Pete St John*

## The Fields Of Athenry

*Written by Pete St John*

I wrote 'The Fields Of Athenry' back in 1970. I had been doing some research in University College Galway, *as Gaeilge*, and I'd been reading about tragic conditions and situations in Athenry, about all the stories of work-houses and times past and I came up with the idea of a young couple, Michael and Mary and their unborn child, and what life might have been like for them.

'The Fields Of Athenry' was the result, and I gave it to Danny Doyle, who was one of the leading artists in the country at the time. He took it to America with him, and it became a major hit. Then I gave it to Paddy Reilly who told me that he was getting out of the game and that 'The Fields Of Athenry' would be his swansong – that was back in 1982! It has now been recorded by over 520 artists. It's been performed by a wide range of people, from James Last to Ted Kennedy, who apparently sings it as his party piece and it's been adopted as the theme tune for Celtic supporters.

## The Fields Of Athenry

*By a lonely prison wall*
*I heard a young girl calling*
*Michael they are taking you away*
*For you stole Trevelyn's corn*
*So the young might see the morn*
*Now a prison ship lies waiting in the bay.*

**Chorus**
*Low lie the fields of Athenry*
*Where once we watched the small free birds fly.*
*Our love was on the wing*
*We had dreams and songs to sing*
*It's so lonely round the fields of Athenry.*

*By a lonely prison wall*
*I heard a young man calling*
*Nothing matters Mary when you're free,*
*Against the Famine and the Crown*
*I rebelled they ran me down*
*Now you must raise our child with dignity.*

**Chorus**
*Low lie the fields of Athenry*
*Where once we watched the small free birds fly.*
*Our love was on the wing*
*We had dreams and songs to sing*
*It's so lonely 'round the fields of Athenry.*

*By a lonely harbour wall*
*She watched the last star falling*
*As that prison ship sailed out against the sky*
*Sure she'll wait and hope and pray*

*For her love in Botany Bay*
*It's so lonely 'round the fields of Athenry.*

**Chorus**
*Low lie the fields of Athenry*
*Where once we watched the small free birds fly.*
*Our love was on the wing*
*We had dreams and songs to sing*
*It's so lonely 'round the fields of Athenry.*

## BIOGRAPHY

Pete St John, the composer of many classic folk songs, including 'Dublin In The Rare Auld Times', 'The Ferryman', 'Moonshine' and 'Strawberry Beds', is a Dubliner through and through.

He was a pupil of Scoil Mhuire Gan Smal, Inchicore and Synge Street CBS and on leaving school emigrated to Canada. He subsequently moved on to Alaska, Central America and the West Indies, where he spent time as a professional athelete, truck driver, logging-camp labourer, PR/sales official and, finally, an electrical contracting executive in the USA.

He became deeply involved in the peace movement and international civil rights before returning to Dublin in the late 1970s.

On his return, he was struck by the changes in his home environment, and this was the catalyst for his distinctive style of writing. Through his words and music, he was able to describe the social conditions around him.

Soon, the major folk artists in Ireland became aware of his talent and those who have gone on to record his compositions include The Dubliners, James Last, Paddy Reilly, Frank Patterson, Danny Doyle, Johnny McEvoy, Mary Black, Lorraine O'Reilly, The Dublin City Ramblers, Luke Kelly, The Bards, Tony Malone, Ronnie Drew, The Barleycorn, The Whole Shebang, Irish Breakdown, Celtic Thunder, Shay Hennessy, Moonshine, Celtic Folk, Noel Nash, Sonny Noels, Brendan Shine, Daniel O'Donnell, Mary Duff, The Three Tenors, John McDermot, Frank Emerson, Jim McCann, Denis

Murray, Maureen Potter, Rakish Paddy, Brendan Grace, Sean Dunphy, Brendan Bowyer and Patsy Watchorn.

Pete's contribution to the folk scene has been acknowledged by his peers both at home and abroad with awards of merit from the Irish Republic Music Writers, the Irish Association of Songwriters and Composers, the US Irish Cultural Society and the US Brendan Cup Committee.

*Jack L*

# Rooftop Lullaby

*Written by Jack L*

*Taken from the album* Metropolis Blue

'Rooftop Lullaby' is one of my personal favourite songs that I've ever written. A lot of songs just appear out of mid-air and, in some sense, 'Rooftop' did just that, but I can also trace its very essence.

I think I was in third class in the local convent school in Athy, County Kildare. I'm not too sure how old I was, probably about eight, I imagine. We were taught a poem called 'I Wonder', by whom, I can't recall. To the best of my memory, it went something like, 'I wonder why the grass is green and why the wind is never seen. Who taught the birds to build their nests and told the trees to take a rest? And when the moon's not quite so round, where can the missing bit be found?' – that's about all I can remember clearly. Well, I've got to tell you, this poem blew the windows off the room that housed my innocent mind. All these crazy questions: who, where, when and why. There is a great quotation by the writer Albert Camus; it goes something like

'Every man's life is a slow trek back to that moment when his imagination was first opened.' I can safely say for me that moment was in that classroom.

So many years and lives later, when my niece Claire was born, the first of the next generation of my family, this poem began to surface again in my consciousness. The wonder of it all. So, one stormy night, I remember sitting alone in my bedsit in Dublin and penning 'Rooftop Lullaby', trying to recapture the heart of the 'I Wonder' poem and the soul of innocence, how children's questions are not as absurd as we often like to think they are. Great wisdom and simplicity can be found in the Zen-like mind of a child.

'Rooftop Lullaby' went further, I suppose, in questioning 'Why do people pass away?' which is a line that especially strikes a chord with those who are grieving. Often people come up to me and say how the song has comforted them, which is pretty much the greatest inspiration to write – thinking you may be comforting or helping someone somewhere.

### Rooftop Lullaby

*Mother is there something in the sky?*
*Something up there that they hide?*
*A jewel for me and you, apple trees with fallen fruit?*
*Daughter now I don't know but I believe,*
*That its beauty's beyond words*
*It's like a tune that I can't sing*
*But I've heard it sung by birds.*
*It's a rooftop lullaby*
*Fallen from the sky*
*Sends us to sleep tonight*
*It's the apple in your eye*
*Keeps you as sweet as pie*
*Dreaming through the night*
*Father won't you tell me if you know,*
*Where does half of the moon go?*
*When it's not up in the sky*

*it disappears before my eyes.*
*Oh my son why does morning break each day?*
*Why do people pass away?*
*Oh its the mystery and truth,*
*it's the innocence in youth.*
*A rooftop lullaby*
*Fallen from the sky*
*Sends us to sleep tonight*
*It's the apple in your eye*
*Keeps you as sweet as pie*
*Dreaming through the night*
*a rooftop lullaby*
*Fallen from the sky*
*Sends us to sleep tonight.*

## BIOGRAPHY

Originally from Athy, County Kildare, Jack Lukeman spent his formative years experimenting with singing and exploring the realms of music. He soon discovered that he could fill large empty spaces with his soaring voice, and this prompted him to write his own material.

He travelled to Europe for a while and became so enamoured with the work and life of the Belgian songwriter Jacques Brel that on the twenty-fifth anniversary of the composer's death, he honoured him with a special show entitled Chez Jack L: Love, Sex, Death & Brel. The show was launched in Dublin's Spirit venue and, though initially scheduled for a three-week run, it went on to do fourteen weeks, performing to over 70,000 people in total.

This influence of Brel saw him explore his own journey through words and music and, on his return to Ireland, he began to carve out a career for himself, progressing from an independent singer to a multi-platinum-selling singer-songwriter of albums such as *Universe* and *Metropolis Blue*, the latter which was hailed by *Hot Press* magazine as 'a timeless collection of fine songs, beautifully delivered from an artist as unique as Ireland has ever produced'.

Jack's voice has been described as 'a mixture of all the great male singing voices of the twentieth century', and he has been compared to and inspired by Scott Walker, Frank Sinatra, Jim Morrison and Tom Waits.

Jack has been recording and touring with a new acoustic-based solo show. He has performed to sell-out crowds on the Guinness Fleadh Festival tour of America and is also one of only a few artists to have performed at the Glastonbury Festival for three consecutive days.

Tim Jarvis

*Hazel O'Connor*

## Rebecca

*Written by Hazel O'Connor*

*Taken from the album* 5 in the Morning

I'd like to pick the song 'Rebecca'. I wrote it in 1995 for my friend Rebecca. She was a hairdresser and I knew her from before I became famous. We shared many similarities in life. In later life, she and her husband split up and she turned to Buddhism. I had different religious beliefs, but while some of our other friends would laugh and say, 'What are you going on about now?' Rebecca and I always respected each other's beliefs and philosophies.

We always had a dream that one day we would have a huge party with an orchestra and music, and we would talk about it every time I went to her to get my hair done. Her life began to get a little better, things improved and the fashion icon Jeff Banks helped her to open a new hairdressing salon but, just three months into her new venture, she collapsed and was taken to hospital. She was told she had an aggressive form of cancer and didn't have long to live. I didn't get to visit her at this time because she didn't want to see anyone; she didn't want her friends to see her when she was sick, and I understood and respected her wishes. We talked on the phone and wrote to each other instead. There were lots of issues going on, but she had so little energy that she wanted to save it for those really closest to her.

After she died, I went through a very angry phase. I was angry at the machinery of God, my marriage broke up and I didn't think life was fair. I was obsessed with grief and anger, to the point where I could barely leave the house. Eventually, I realised it was crazy and I couldn't live like that any longer. I decided to write this song to help me lighten the load. It was the definitive song about my friend Rebecca, and I used to play it a lot with the band when we were on tour because it went down well with the audience and has a beautiful chorus.

Later on, I decided to try to redefine my career, and myself and the band recorded an acoustic version of 'Rebecca'. It brought me a great level of success and I performed it at all the major festivals. Of all the songs I have written, I think it moves people the most. People often cry when they hear it, but I don't think that's a bad thing. I think the song unlocks something inside of them and I feel proud that I have facilitated that. It gives me a strange pleasure knowing that I reach people and that, in turn, the audience touch their friends in some small way. I don't believe that we are in tune with the echoes and spirit-natures of ourselves enough. I hope that I can help other people through this song and in a strange way I can reach out and touch Rebecca, and keep a little part of her with me.

## Rebecca

*A top flat in Bayswater, Rebecca would be doing my hair,*
*We had so much fun she sang all of the words to my song,*
*As it played on the player.*
*She'd give me her bed for the night, she would feed me and clothe me and such,*
*I'd laugh and say, when the light hits that way,*
*You remind me of Shirley MacLaine.*

**Chorus**
*When will I see you again?*
*When will we sing silly harmonies into the night?*
*I try and try but I can't help missing you,*
*I wonder where you are now.*

*We had us a dream back then, when we got back the things that were stole,*
*We'd have an old fashioned party, an orchestra, long gowns,*
*And we'd be the belles of the ball,*
*And we'd dance to the Emperor's Waltz, because that was her favourite song*
*I'd laugh and say, when the light hits that way,*
*You remind me of Shirley MacLaine.*

**Chorus**
*When will I see you again?*
*When will we sing silly harmonies into the night?*
*I try and try but I can't help missing you,*
*I wonder where you are now.*

*Are you an angel, have you been reborn?*
*Did you find your Buddha, was it worth all the toil?*
*I write this 'cause I miss you and there's nothing more I can do.*

**Chorus**
*When will I see you again?*
*When will we sing silly harmonies into the night?*
*I try and try but I can't help missing you,*
*I wonder where you are now.*

*Now the top flat is empty, but our rare old times call from the walls,*
*And I hope that wherever you are you're all right.*
*And I'll still have our ball,*
*And we'll dance to the Emperor's Waltz because that was your favourite tune*
*I'd laugh and say, when the light hits that way,*
*You remind me of Shirley MacLaine.*

**Chorus**

*When will I see you again?*
*When will we sing silly harmonies into the night?*
*I try and try but I can't help missing you,*
*I wonder where you are now.*

## BIOGRAPHY

Hazel O'Connor was born in Coventry, England, but now lives in County Wicklow. Her life story is chequered and intriguing, and many of her past experiences are expressed in her music.

She left home at just sixteen and lived in a squat in Amsterdam before travelling to Morocco and Japan where she worked as a dancer. She encountered difficulties on her next journey in Beirut when civil war broke out. She returned to London, unsure of her life's direction, and opted for singing and songwriting.

Hazel got her big break when director Brian Gibson chose her to star in the film *Breaking Glass*, alongside Phil Daniels, Jim Broadbent and Jonathan Price. This saw her take the Variety Club of Great Britain's 1980 Film Actress of the Year award, and she was also nominated for Best Newcomer. Hazel single-handedly wrote and performed all the songs for the film, and the best-selling album, produced by Tony Visconti, was also nominated for the Best Film Soundtrack BAFTA.

Her next album *Sons and Lovers* gave rise to the hit song 'Decadent Days' (aka 'D-Days'), which she performed to an enthusiastic audience on *Top of the Pops*. However, financial difficulties arose and threatened the success she had created. It appeared that the all-important contracts that Hazel had signed with her label and publisher were fundamentally flawed, and, despite the millions of records sold, she was headed for bankruptcy.

Nevertheless, her spirit and determination shone through, and she turned to acting, with a role alongside Derek Thompson in the BBC drama series *Fighting Back*. The series received rave reviews, giving Hazel some much needed security and enabling her to start afresh in the USA where she married and continued a blossoming career. She settled in Ireland in the early 1990s.

It was around this time that she signed a new deal with Sony, Germany, and went on to record three albums *To Be Free*, *Over the Moon* and *Private Wars*, which attracted great success in Germany, France and throughout Europe. When the deal expired, she independently recorded the *Live in Berlin* album followed by a new studio album, *Five in the Morning*. After the last big-band tour in 1998 to promote this album, her close friend Herbie Flowers encouraged her to tell her life story in a show and so *Beyond Breaking Glass*, the show, was born. The production saw Hazel collaborate with celebrated Irish harpist Cormac De Barra, and the show played to critical acclaim all over Europe as well as in the USA and Australia. From the show's success, an album of the same name was made.

Hazel released her first ever 'Best of', *A Singular Collection*, at the end of 2003. This was closely followed by a cover of George Michael's 'One More Try' in March 2004.

The album *Hidden Heart*, sees Hazel working with producer Martin Rushent. It was released in May 2005 and is a valuable culmination of all her work to date, bringing her into contact again with celebrated harpist Cormac De Barra in a unique musical marriage.

*Liam Lawton*

## The Cloud's Veil

*Written by Liam Lawton*

*Taken from the album* Another World

I wrote 'The Cloud's Veil' shortly after an uncle of mine had been killed in a car crash on the Naas Road. He was a great music mentor of mine and we used to play together a lot. We were actually due to play together around the time of his death. For a long time after he died, I was very down and I didn't write at all, and then one day someone sent me a card and there were two simple lines on it which read, 'When the sun is veiled from the sky remember I am still there' — that gave me the inspiration for writing this song.

I wrote the piece and included it in my repertoire. Then, the day after 9/11, my publishers in the USA called me to say that the people who were organising a memorial service for the victims of that day were looking for a piece of music to use and they had narrowed it down to three songs, 'Be Not Afraid', 'Amazing Grace' and 'The Cloud's Veil', and they decided to run with mine. I think they felt the words were appropriate given the images in their minds: 'when the dark clouds veil the sky, I am by your side'.

They asked me if I would allow the song to be downloaded for free, which I readily agreed to. In that first hour alone, there were over 1,000 downloads – all across America – and it was performed at a lot of the funerals of the victims of 9/11. When something like that happens, it seems to take on a life of its own outside of my own involvement. I found it amazing that something that came out of my own personal grief could help so many other people through theirs.

There is another story to this song too. I was teaching in a school in the Bronx in New York, and, late at night one Christmas, there were children there who still hadn't been collected by their parents. The teachers divided the kids up between them. One of the young fellows was waiting for his mother to come and collect him, but there had been a car crash and she had been killed, and we had to tell him that she wasn't coming home. I remember for months afterwards the sound of him crying that night; it was very sad. I used to think about him a lot and, nine months later, I was mowing the grass at home in Carlow when I received a letter. It had been redirected three times but it got to me eventually. It was actually from the teacher in this school, and he said that they had wanted to write to the composer of that song because they had used it in the healing process for this young boy so that was also a nice response to the song.

### The Cloud's Veil

> *Even though the rain hides the stars,*
> *Even though the mist swirls the hills,*
> *Even when the dark clouds veil the sky,*
> *You are by my side.*

***Chorus***

*Even when the sun shall fall in sleep,*
*Even when at dawn the sky shall weep,*
*Even in the night when storms shall rise,*
*You are by my side, you are by my side.*

*Bright the stars at night,*
*That mirror Heaven's way to you.*
*Bright the stars in light,*
*Where dwell the saints in love and truth.*

***Chorus***

*Even when the sun shall fall in sleep,*
*Even when at dawn the sky shall weep,*
*Even in the night when storms shall rise,*
*You are by my side, you are by my side.*

*Held in memory,*
*The thoughts we have of yesterday,*
*May our future be,*
*A resting place where love will stay.*

*Even though the rain hides the stars.*

## BIOGRAPHY

The last two years have been arguably the most hectic of Liam Lawton's career. He signed to EMI Music, went into studio to record a new album and undertook two major sell-out Irish tours. His highly acclaimed album *Another World* entered the album chart at No. 7 with double-platinum sales of almost 40,000. The summer of 2005 saw him working with the talents of the world-renowned Czech Philharmonic Chamber Orchestra for his new album *Time*, which was recorded mainly in Prague. This was produced by

Mark Cahill, with orchestral arrangements handled by the highly acclaimed Chicago Symphony Orchestra arranger Gary Fry.

Liam showed the first signs of what was to become a major part of his life in early childhood when he became an accomplished piano player with a special interest in Irish traditional music. He went on to study arts in Maynooth College, and this provided him with a golden opportunity to put his songwriting abilities to the test by entering the college's annual song contest, which he subsequently won on three consecutive occasions, and also winning the Ballina Song Contest on his first attempt, which attracted major interest from record companies all over Ireland.

However, music wasn't the only love in Liam's life, and it was around this time that he decided to study for the priesthood. For the next seven years, he devoted himself entirely to the Church and undertook pastoral work in Carlow town, which meant that music was put on the backburner.

But as Liam might say himself, 'God works in mysterious ways,' and he found a way to combine both passions. One year, the organisers of the Arts Festival in Carlow found themselves without their special guest performer, Peadar O'Riada. They asked Liam if he would mind standing in and playing some of Peadar's material. He agreed but asked if he could play his own material – they agreed, and he took to the stage for the first time in seven years, immediately tasting and savouring the hunger for performing music once again and casting aside any doubts about an imminent return to music.

An Bord Gaeilge subsequently offered him a grant to record a collection of liturgical music in the Irish language. This was distributed through Veritas, the religious store in Dublin. They then set up a deal with Liam to record an album of his music in English, and this became an instant best-seller.

On Liam's return to Carlow, he completed a H.Dip. in teaching, whilst writing and recording music in his spare time. In 1996, he was commissioned by Trócaire to write a music piece commemorating the 150th anniversary of the Irish Famine. The result, 'The Darkest Hour', was brought to the attention of the World Health Organisation in the USA. He subsequently performed the song at the opening of a special commemoration exhibition of the Irish Famine in Minneapolis, and this, in turn, led to him being offered a publishing deal by GIA Publications, a major Christian music publishing company who were captivated by his liturgical music writing.

In 2000, he was approached by Siamsa na nGael, a committee set up to promote Irish Culture in Chicago, to write a work for their St Patrick's Night celebrations the following year. This night is a huge focus for the Irish-American community in Chicago, and for this Liam wrote 'The Shepherd Boy', which tells the story of the life of St Patrick. With Gregory Peck handling narration duties, Mo' Tenor Rod Dixon on vocals and a beautiful performance from the Chicago Symphony Orchestra, the evening was a resounding success and catapulted Liam Lawton on to the international stage.

After contributing 'The Cloud's Veil' to the grieving US people in the aftermath of 9/11, Liam took a career break from teaching to do a masters degree in World Music, studying under Micheál Ó'Súilleabháin, from which he emerged with first-class honours.

Following the success of 'The Shepherd Boy' in Chicago on St Patrick's Day 2001, he returned to the same venue in 2003 to perform a new piece of work based on the life of St Brigid. He was joined by Joan Cusack on narration and Aidan Conway on vocals.

His career continued to go from strength to strength, prompting him to set up his own vocal/instrumental group for touring purposes entitled Lorica. This union led to a very special performance in the Vatican, undoubtedly one of the highlights of his career.

By 2004, Liam had been offered a major recording deal with EMI Records. He released a number of albums including *Light the Fire, In the Quiet, Cloud's Veil, Ancient Ways, Future Days: A Celtic Season of Songs, A Day of Our Own: Music for a Wedding Liturgy* and *Another World*, collaborating with guest artists Brian Kennedy, The Celtic Tenors, Róisín O'Reilly, Fionnuala Sherry, Eimear Quinn and Moya Brennan along the way.

*Luka Bloom*

## The Man Is Alive

*Written by Luka Bloom*
*Taken from the album* Riverside

About eighteen years ago, I was on tour in North America, and, for some reason, I'd been thinking about my father a lot that year. He had died in 1956 when I was eighteen months old.

While I was in Vancouver in 1988, I met a young woman, who brought me to a Native American park beside the city. As we looked at the city and the water, she pointed to the village in the mountains where she had grown up. She talked about her family and about her father, who had also died suddenly when she was just eighteen months old. We talked and talked for hours, and during our talk, I felt a gorgeous new connection with my father, which literally changed my life.

Soon I wrote 'The Man Is Alive', the song I regard as the most important of my life.

## The Man Is Alive

*The man is alive.*
*The night sometimes seems dangerous,*
*We wonder what it hides.*
*It sometimes brings us closer,*
*And forever changes our lives.*
*Strangers talk in open ways,*
*We cannot always understand,*
*Who have not felt the loving touch,*
*And seen the guiding hand.*

*I was brought up near the riverside,*
*In a quiet Irish town.*
*An eighteen-month-old baby,*
*The night they laid my daddy down,*
*Everyone knew everyone,*
*And everybody else as well,*
*My home was filled with sorrow then,*
*Too much for me to tell.*

*Chorus*
*The man is alive,*
*Alive and breathing,*
*It's taken me so long to see,*
*The man is alive,*
*Alive and breathing,*
*The man is alive in me,*
*The man is alive in me.*

*We stood among the totem poles,*
*Under the Canadian moonlight,*
*She told me all about her childhood days,*
*On the Vancouver mountain side.*

*An eighteen-month-old baby.*
*The night her daddy passed away,*
*We stood and watched the darkness,*
*Flowing into the light of day.*

*The night sometimes seems dangerous,*
*We wonder what it hides.*
*It sometimes brings us close,*
*And for ever changed our lives.*
*Strangers talk in open ways,*
*We cannot always understand,*
*But we begin to feel the loving touch,*
*And see the guiding hand.*

***Chorus***
*The man is alive,*
*Alive and breathing,*
*It's taken me so long to see,*
*The man is alive,*
*Alive and breathing,*
*The man is alive in me.*

## BIOGRAPHY

Luka Bloom (aka Barry Moore) was born in Moorefield, Newbridge, County Kildare, and came from a family of strong singers and songwriters. He first embarked on his musical journey when he toured the pubs and clubs of England with his brother Christy Moore.

In 1987, Barry flew to America and, by the time he arrived back on Irish soil, he had reinvented himself as Luka Bloom. He had performed his own compositions to captive audiences around the USA, gigging with The Pogues, The Violent Femmes, The Dixie Chicks, The Hothouse Flowers and The Cowboy Junkies. He signed with Warner Music in Los Angeles and made *Riverside*, *The Acoustic Motorbike* and *Turf*.

He made *Salty Heaven* in Birr, County Offaly, in 1997. He had read about the American folk singer Ani DiFranco and her independent crusade to make her own music in her own way, in her own time, released by her own people. This concept was one that appealed to him greatly, and he set about establishing his own independent way of working – 2000 saw him record *Keeper of the Flame*, an album of eclectic covers by great artists.

In 2001, he created Big Sky Records and launched his own website www.lukabloom.com. He also released *The Barry Moore Years*, an album of self-penned songs pre-1987. The year 2001 also saw the composition of *Between the Mountains and the Moon*, an album of new and original songs, and in 2003, *Amsterdam* was released – a rousing live performance from a great night in the Carré Theatre in Amsterdam. In 2004 he recorded *Before Sleep Comes*.

His album *Innocence,* released in 2005, has been well received worldwide and brings the listener on an enchanting journey from Chicago to Fanore, exploring such topics as music, war and love along the way.

*Kieran Goss*

## Reasons To Leave (Heaven On Earth)

*Written by Kieran Goss and Rodney Crowell*
*Taken from the album* Red-Letter Day

The song I'd like to pick is 'Reasons To Leave (Heaven On Earth)'. I co-wrote it with a good friend of mine, Rodney Crowell – Rodney loved the title 'Heaven On Earth' and I loved the title 'Reasons To Leave' so we combined the two!

I had the melody for 'Reasons To Leave' in my head for a couple of years, as well as the title, and I had tried numerous times to write the lyrics.

I come from Newry, from a large family of fifteen children, and I knew first-hand the whole experience of people emigrating to find work. Newry was a real blackspot in terms of finding employment and I had older brothers and sisters who went off to the USA and Canada – even now I have brothers and sisters still living in Toronto and some in London, so I wanted to write a song about emigration, but I wanted to write one that was from a personal point of view. In Irish folk music in particular, there are a lot of songs about emigration, and some of them are great but some are clichéd, and I really wanted to avoid the clichés – so I had a go at writing the words myself over a period of time. I knew the melody was great, and I knew the title was great and the idea, but two or three times I wrote lyrics and then discarded them because, although they were good songs, they weren't exactly what I wanted.

Then, about five or six years ago, I met Rodney Crowell, and you know when you meet someone and you just click? You know that you have the same sense of humour and the same approach to writing – you feel a connection.

We were sitting in a hotel in Galway talking, and I was telling him about my family and my background, and he was telling me about his parents and his grandparents who had gone to live in Texas – and I suddenly realised that the conversation we were having *was* the song, so I asked him what he thought of the idea and the melody and he loved it.

Sometimes some of these songwriting conferences are almost *too* professional, and people try too hard to write a hit. I told him I didn't know if anyone would ever record the song again but that it was a really important song for me to do. So, after circling around the song for a number of years, we just sat there together and wrote it in about two hours.

I personally think that it's my best song, even though it is a very emotional one for me to sing, and I couldn't perform it for a year and a half after writing it because there is a lot of stuff in it, particularly relevant to my family. It is close to the bone.

What both Rodney and I love about it is that it is one of those songs that even though it's universal, it is also personal to a lot of people. In a really freaky way, even though songs like 'Out Of My Head' have been bigger hits and have been recorded loads of times, 'Reasons To Leave' has been recorded by about twenty different people in lots of different languages, so in its own quiet way, it went out there into the world and has emigrated itself!

It's a song that I'm very proud of, and I have performed it everywhere from Nashville to New Zealand, and I've seen how people react to it; I've seen people almost crying when I play it, so it works on lots of levels and for that reason I would choose it as my most important song.

## Reasons To Leave (Heaven On Earth)

*Ireland's a dream,*
*Of hope for what the day will bring,*
*The land and the sea,*
*Is what I've come to trust,*
*All that I am,*
*Is telling me I should not go,*
*And all that I know,*
*Is they're telling me I must.*

*Reasons to leave,*
*Are money and finding better work,*
*Reasons to stay,*
*Are music and love.*
*Reasons to leave,*
*Are fortune and fame for what it's worth.*
*The reason to stay,*
*Is heaven on earth.*

*My brothers are ten,*
*And sisters I have five.*
*Four to one bed,*
*Is room enough to grow.*
*All that we are,*
*Is all that I have ever known,*
*And all that I have,*
*Will be here when I'm gone.*

*I've heard about work up in Boston,*
*Laying tracks down to San Augustine,*
*Sometimes with an eye for New Zealand,*
*I lean.*

# BIOGRAPHY

Just how singer-songwriter Kieran Goss managed to find any time to himself to indulge his musical desires as a young boy growing up in County Down is hard to fathom, with fourteen brothers and sisters to distract him. But whether it was to escape into a little private world created for himself, or to entertain the troops, is irrelevant – he did so in style and created a loyal fan base in the process.

Kieran was born and raised in Newry and got his first guitar at just nine years of age. With sixteen other people in the house, musical tastes were wide and varied and, as a youngster, he was raised on a diverse diet of Johnny Cash, Kris Kristofferson, Willie Nelson, Frank Sinatra and the Rolling Stones. Such varied tastes somehow fermented to give him his own unique sound.

Kieran juggled his legal studies in Belfast with playing gigs in Queen's University Students' Union, eventually working his way up the ladder until he was supporting Elvis Costello, Christy Moore and Joe Jackson.

He went on to qualify as a lawyer in the mid-1980s, but the lure of adventure saw him leave his native land and travel around France and Germany, playing music all the way. He returned home in 1989 and recorded his first album *Brand New Star*.

The *New Day* album followed in 1994 and, four years later, came *Worse than Pride*, which featured the Top 10 hit 'Out Of My Head'. This went on to become the second most played song on Irish radio that year. *Worse than Pride* achieved double-platinum status nine months after it was released. *Red-Letter Day* followed in 2000, which features 'Reasons To Leave'.

In 2002, Kieran released the compilation, *Out of my Head – The Best of Kieran Goss*, which gave him time to work on his sixth studio album, *Blue Sky Sunrise*. This was recorded in Tennessee in 2005 and was produced by Rodney Crowell and Peter Coleman. 'Clear Day' was the first single released from the album and was followed by an Irish tour.

## Maura O'Connell

### Time To Learn

*Written by Tim O'Brien* and *Pat Alger*
*Taken from the album* Don't I Know

Any song worth its salt, like any great poem, can speak to – or for – everyone.

A feeling of personal connection to a song, shaped by a person's frame of mind the first time they hear it, can last a lifetime.

I first heard 'Time to Learn' by Tim O'Brien and Pat Alger not long after my mother had passed away, very suddenly, in 1988. I remember vividly the first night I heard it. It was at a gig Tim was doing at the Station Inn in Nashville. I felt like he had somehow peered into my soul and saw that I needed a place to put some of the shock and pain that I had been carrying around with me.

I cried and cried from the very first line, until the song was over and for a long time afterwards.

After that, every time I went to hear Tim, I would ask him to sing it. Now that I, myself, perform the song, I know it is very hard to just randomly place it in a set-list – but, more often than not, Tim would oblige and I would bawl my head off all over again!

I told Tim, after every performance he did, that as soon as I could listen to the song without falling apart, I was going to record it.

It was thirteen years before I was ready.

It became the cornerstone of my album *Don't I Know*.

I knew it couldn't be slipped, at random, into a 'regular' song selection, so when it came time to do the record, it felt right because that record really is about the realities of middle-age experiences, the biggest of which is the loss of parents. I made sure to sing it for my sisters, none of whom allowed me to get beyond the first verse and chorus before begging me to stop.

It had hit them the same way that it had hit me. I find that audiences react the same way. I can hear the sound of muffled crying out in the audience.

A song like that gives us a safe place to articulate feelings that are deep and painful, and the fact that the words were written by another human shows us that we are not alone in our pain.

### Time To Learn

*The hand is cold that once held mine*
*I can't believe you've really left this world behind*
*I can wait, I can hope*
*I'll get over this in time*

*It takes time to learn when someone's gone for good*
*They're not coming back like you wish they would*
*In the empty hours when you miss them so*
*It takes time to learn to let them go*

*Your last hours we never knew*
*We never had the chance to say goodbye to you*
*Words unsaid, things undone*
*We'd just begun and now we'll never see them through*

*It takes time to learn when someone's gone for good*
*They're not coming back like you wish they would*
*In the empty hours when you miss them so*
*It takes time to learn to let them go*

## BIOGRAPHY

Maura O'Connell is a native of County Clare and was destined for a musical career, if the influence of her mother was anything to go by. She and her three sisters would often sing together at home, and her mother's love of opera wafted through the house. As she grew older, Maura became interested in folk music and joined the tradition-oriented Celtic band Dé Danann, a move that was instrumental in her eventual interest in the experimental roots music of America's New Grass Revival.

In 1986, she travelled to Nashville to pursue her dream and her collaborations with new grass masters such as banjoist Bela Fleck and dobro stylist Jerry Douglas provided valuable material for a lot of her recorded work – including the Grammy-nominated *Helpless Heart* and *Blue Is the Color of Hope* for Warner Bros, *Stories* and the Irish-oriented *Wandering Home* for Hannibal/Rykodisc, and *Walls and Windows* and *Don't I Know* for Sugar Hill.

Over the years, Maura has covered compositions from some of the best in the business, including Mary Chapin Carpenter, Shawn Colvin, John Gorka, Patty Griffin, Jim Lauderdale, Kim Richey, Leslie Satcher, Ron Sexsmith, Mindy Smith and Cheryl Wheeler.

Somehow, Maura manages to own each song she sets her voice to, the melody lingering in the air long after the music has faded away.

Her albums include *Maura O'Connell: Just in Time*, *Always*, *Helpless Heart*, *A Real Life Story*, *Blue Is the Colour of Hope*, *Stories*, *Wandering Home*, *Walls and Windows* and her most recent album *Don't I Know*. She also features on *A Woman's Heart* and *A Woman's Heart 2*.

*Michael McGlynn — Anúna*

## Where All Roses Go

*Written by Michael McGlynn. Text adapted from Francis Ledwidge's poems*
*'Lament for Thomas MacDonagh' and 'June'*
*Taken from the album* Behind the Closed Eye

The song I have chosen is actually an amalgamation of two poems by the poet Francis Ledwidge who died in 1917 – one is called 'June' and the other is 'Lament for Thomas MacDonagh'. It's from the album *Behind the Closed Eye,* and I wrote it in 1997.

The basis of why the piece was written is that I was commissioned to write an orchestral work by the Ulster Orchestra in Belfast. I had already written a number of pieces for them, and, coincidentally, a couple of years earlier I had done a concert in the Queen Elizabeth Hall in London with Jeff Buckley. I had been asked by Elvis Costello to sing as part of this concert and had heard Jeff on television only a week before.

When Jeff died in 1997, he was only thirty (which was the age Francis Ledwidge was when he died), and he died while I was writing this song, so the whole concept of the song changed.

The poem was something that was supposed to be influenced by nature and by Ledwidge's view on being in a straight line from the nature poets of the medieval Irish past, but it actually turned into one of the hardest songs I've ever had to write because it was deeply upsetting and moving. It's interesting for a composer to look at a text and get a resonance for the words and then simply set the text to music, but, in this case, I had started to do that and suddenly I was influenced by something which was difficult in a personal way. Jeff died way too early, and he only produced one album – an extraordinary one called *Grace* – and it deeply affected me at that time.

When you write music, it is very much dictated by the heart, and that single song is probably the reason I have not really produced much work since because it's very difficult to be sincere and honest and open through music without actually feeling something inside that enables you to transmit that to other people.

## Where All Roses Go

*He shall not hear the bittern cry,*
*In the wild sky, where he is lain,*
*Nor voices of the sweeter birds,*
*Above the wailing of the rain.*

*Nor shall he know when loud March blows,*
*Thro' slanting snows her fanfare shrill,*
*Blowing to flame the golden cup,*
*Of many an upset daffodil.*

*But when the Dark Cow leaves the moor,*
*And pastures poor with greedy weeds,*
*Perhaps he'll hear her low at morn,*
*Lifting her horn in pleasant meads.*

*Soon the swallows will be flying south,*
*The wind wheel north to gather in the snow,*
*Even the roses split on youth's red mouth,*
*Will soon blow down the road all roses go.*

*Dedicated to Jeff Buckley (1967-1997)*

# BIOGRAPHY

Michael McGlynn was born in Dublin and is best known as composer for and director of the hugely successful Irish choir Anúna, which he founded in 1987. It wasn't always an easy road, but Anúna have made their mark and have gone from strength to strength. They have released nine albums since 1993, almost exclusively featuring Michael's arrangements and original works.

Anúna's *Deep Dead Blue* was the first Irish record to be nominated for a Classical Brit Award and went into the Top 5 in the UK classical charts. *Essential Anúna,* featuring Michael's original works and arrangements, was released by Universal UK in 2003, where it charted in the classical charts and, in 2005, it was released by Koch International Records in the USA.

Currently, many hundreds of choral groups worldwide perform Michael's work on a regular basis, with some of his pieces entering the choral venacular as standards, including the piece 'Dúlamán', which has been recorded many times, in particular by the Grammy Award winning US all-male vocal group Chanticleer, who have commissioned a new work from Michael for performance in 2007.

Finnish vocal group Rajaton have also performed and recorded his work, and he has written specially commissioned vocal works for many international groups. Michael has written a large number of instrumental and orchestral works which have been performed worldwide. His saxophone and piano work 'Visions', commissioned by Gerard McCrystal in 1996, has been particularly successful and is on the syllabus of the Royal College of Music in London.

His music can be heard on film and television soundtracks all over the world, including on the award-winning film *The Work of Angels*, which is an exploration of the *Book of Kells*. His collaborative project, *Silver River,* for orchestra and oboe (commissioned by oboist Matthew Manning), features an entire album of his original work and arrangements, while *Behind the Closed Eye*, originally premiered and recorded by the Ulster Orchestra and Anúna, is currently being adapted as an orchestral and vocal suite.

Michael was musical director for the historic Adrian Noble/Cusack Family production of Chekov's *Three Sisters* at the Gate Theatre Dublin and Royal Court London, and was commissioned to write an original score for the play. He acted again as musical director for Jim Sheridan's production of *The Risen People* at Dublin's Gaiety Theatre. He is an accomplished solo singer, specialising in early music and has worked with many international artists as a soloist including, most notably, Elvis Costello, Fretwork and Jeff Buckley. He has written songs with country-music legends Rodney Crowell and Delbert McClinton and has also written a number of songs with his twin brother John.

Anúna's new album, *Sensation*, was released in 2006.

*Dominic Kirwan*

## Absent Friends

*Written by Duncan McCrone and Cy Jack*
*Taken from the album* Golden Dreams

Many of the songs I sing have literally been handed to me in their infancy, and what I see in them can be something completely different to what the composor sees, but when I perform 'Absent Friends', I find that the audience really responds to it. I can see that they are taking different meanings from it. Some of them are literally thinking about absent friends, some are thinking of family members who are missing, an old schoolfriend or someone who has passed on. Everyone identifies with the lyrics in some way.

It's all to do with how you interpret songs. I'm going into the studio now to record an original song, and I might see something totally different in it to the producer or the writer.

## Absent Friends

*The friends I've lost through growing up,*
*With different roads to try.*
*They've shaken hands and said, 'So long',*
*But really meant goodbye.*
*For if in time, we meet again,*
*The chances are, like strangers we will be.*
*But I remember that we were friends,*
*And they will always be.*

### Chorus
*Here's a toast to absent friends,*
*Wherever they may be.*
*To all I've lost, to absent friends,*
*They're always here with me.*
*If just in memory.*

*The friends I've lost,*
*Through things I've said,*
*And foolish things I've done.*
*They've turned around and walked away,*
*And I miss them every one.*
*What I know now, if I'd known it then,*
*They'd still be here,*
*Here with me today.*
*But I remember that we were friends,*
*And I've thrown it all away.*

### Chorus
*Here's a toast to absent friends,*
*Wherever they may be.*
*To all I've lost, to absent friends,*
*They're always here with me.*
*If just in memory.*

*Instrumental*

*Chorus*
*Here's a toast to absent friends,*
*Wherever they may be.*
*To all I've lost, to absent friends,*
*They're always here with me.*
*If just in memory.*

# BIOGRAPHY

While Dominic enjoys international status today with chart-topping albums and successful concert tours, his Irish roots and early musical influences can still be seen in his live shows.

After several years of performing and developing his own individual style, Dominic was signed to Ritz Records, one of Ireland and the UK's leading independent labels. The first fruits of this relationship was the release of a four-track EP entitled *The Green Hills Are Rolling Still* followed by his debut Ritz album *Try a Little Kindness*. Further albums followed, and firmly established as an artist, headlining his own tours, Dominic not only hosted his own television series but also picked up the prestigious BBC Entertainment Media of the Year Award for Easy Listening/Country Music.

It was his album *On the Way to a Dream,* however, that gave him his first chart-topping success, holding the top spot in the UK country chart. This was followed with the top-selling video, *Dominic Kirwan in Concert*. The release of the compilation *The Very Best of Dominic Kirwan* marked the end of the first chapter of his career and also proved to be the perfect introduction to his music for many new fans.

In 1999, Dominic travelled to Nashville, where he collaborated with some of Nashville's best-known musicians, under the production of Ronnie Light. This saw the birth of the *Unconditional Love* album, which once again catapulted Dominic to the top of the British country charts. He returned to Nashville on two more occasions to repeat the winning formula and recorded *Stone in Love With You* and *Under Your Spell* whilst he was there.

Other titles released by Dominic include the videos *Live in Galway* and his television concert special *The Entertainer*. His double CD, *The Very Best of Dominic Kirwan Vol. 2,* was released in 2002, and, in 2003, he released a new album, *Echoes of Ireland*, containing many personal favourites and evocative songs from his youth.

He tours continually and performs up to two hundred shows a year, including a special weekend each year for his most loyal fans – his friends and neighbours in his home town of Omagh.

The future looks very bright for Dominic, and if hard work is a measure for success, then he will continue to be at the top of his game for many years to come.

*Shay Cotter*

## It's The Old World For Me

*Written by Shay Cotter*

*Yet to be released*

First, I'll try to describe the melody of this song before you read the lyrics. I wanted to have some 'old-style' music in keeping with the sentiment of the words. Imagine the bass player sleepily draped over his double bass, cigarette hanging from his mouth (like that guy from The Stranglers) while plucking the notes and turning it into an almost polka-like waltz. The lead-guitar player tries his hand at some Turkish-style riffs that would sound better on a mandolin of course, and the fiddle player pulls off some sneaky Gypsy-style runs. Now you're half-way there.

Often when I'm writing a song, I'll try to create a character so the song is not necessarily about myself. In one song, 'A Pair Of Dice', a guy travels the world and gets by with just a pair of dice and his wits. 'When I Was A Millionaire' describes someone discovering that perhaps it's the free things in life that are priceless.

In 'It's The Old World For Me', we find a guy yearning for the old way of life; it's likely he has come to accept that it doesn't exist anymore and never will again, but he can still talk and dream about it.

There are many things mentioned in the song that have long since vanished. No one makes a living 'selling blackthorn' anymore, and there's very little 'wayside dancing' taking place now. The 'monorail' train, which was a unique and strange looking contraption, ran between Listowel and Ballybunion for thirty years or so and made its final journey in 1924. Also, the thought of 'swapping stories' by the fireside would be met with consternation nowadays by anyone addicted to their television sets, I'm sure.

My grandparents lived and worked in the USA for many years and returned to Ireland by ship. They treated themselves to one 'luxury' before they left and brought back a Victrola all the way on the boat. This is an old record player that you have to wind up to play. The one they bought was made in 1906, and I marvel at how it still works and plays those old scratchy records even today. They really built things to last long ago and never thought in terms of disposable products.

Time marches on, and everything changes in the name of 'progress', but our friend in this song is defiant. He can close his eyes and dream his way back, or is it possible he can make his mantra a reality?

'It's the old world for me . . . It's the old world for me.'

### It's The Old World For Me

*I want an old Ford or Austin*
*I want to find that big rocking chair*
*I'd like a fireplace that smokes out the house*
*An old stove, a piece of land, a cart and mare*

*To play my Victrola in the pantry*
*We'll run riot in the fields*
*I want tobacco in my pouch*
*I'll hide my money down the couch*

*I guess it's plain to see*
*That it's the old world for me*


*I'd sell blackthorn, gather kindlewood*
*I'd cycle roads that no one ever could*
*In old breeches and my cutaway coat*
*Go catching fish out in my mackerel boat*
*Well I'd be hunting in my hobnailed boots*
*Cook stirabout and peel exotic fruits*
*To be so happy wild and free*
*Just thinking how it all could be.*
*Now it's plain to see that it's the old world for me*

### Bridge
*Wayside dancing at the Ultima Thule*
*There's a race down at the gap of Killarney*
*I want one last trip on that monorail train*
*And a small hip flask for the journey*


*I'd fill the panniers full of turf and straw*
*Build a cottage where I can read and draw*
*My pampooties for a beachside stroll*
*Some Rizla papers for a late night roll*
*I want the fireside to scream and roar*
*We'll swap old stories never heard before*
*A sweet girl sitting on my knee*
*I'd play my banjo with such glee*
*Now you all can see...*
*That it's the old world for me*
*It's the old world for me*
*It's the old world for me*

# BIOGRAPHY

Shay Cotter hails from Celbridge, County Kildare, and first began playing the guitar in his teens. He developed a unique picking style, mixing folk, blues and pop melodies to his poetic and varied lyrics. He made his television debut on the RTÉ show *PM Live,* which led to an invitation to play the Vicar Street venue in Dublin on its opening night, giving him the privilege to be the first person to play there.

In 2000, he recorded an album called *Morning Insomniac* which received high critical acclaim.

When Shay takes to the stage, his songs come alive. His lyrical narration is outstanding, finishing with one sentence and leaving you gasping to hear its conclusion. His highly original ten-minute epic 'Dr Skairee' remains the best example of this. His guitar-playing sounds like a band as he plucks, pulls, hammers and bends every last note to create the illusion of many instruments rolled into one.

The themes of Shay's songs are wide and varied, and he has guested with artists as diverse as David Gray, Jools Holland, The Gypsy Kings, Richie Havens, The Doobie Brothers and The Blind Boys of Alabama to name but a few. In 2002 and 2003, he completed two European tours with fellow songwriter and friend Declan O' Rourke, and he has since toured Ireland regularly. He currently presents his own radio music show, 'Saturday Night Jukebox', every Saturday evening on the new Liffey Station, Sound FM and is also working on demos for his first official CD release.

# Believe

*Damien Dempsey*

## Spraypaint Backalley

*Written by Damien Dempsey*
*Taken from the album* Shots

Usually when I write a song, I write with structure. I try to write two verses and two choruses, but for 'Spraypaint Backalley' I decided I wanted to do something different, and that's how the song came about. It didn't have a chorus and was just very different to the kind of stuff I would usually do.

It's about being a youngster and all the things I saw and the experiences I had while growing up. It's a bit like the music of Planxty – they often started off a song with just one voice or one instrument before building up to something more dramatic, and that's what I do with this song. It lasts right through to the end.

I also wanted to include a favourite quotation of mine from Oscar Wilde, 'We are all in the gutter but some of us are looking at the stars.' That quote really struck a chord with me, and I sing it four times at the end of the song. I often do that, I hear one line or a quotation and it inspires me to write something.

My audiences have always been very receptive to this song and when I sing it, the audience sings the quotation at the end. When you hear thousands of people singing it back at you, it gives you an amazing feeling.

### Spraypaint Backalley

*Down a spraypaint backalley*
*I look up at the sky*
*And I see through red eyes*
*The seagulls wheel around and around*
*Worn out couches and fridges*
*And mongrel dogs roam free*
*There are rags and there are riches*
*Inside this head for me*

*We drink cheap English cider*
*And smoke hashish from North Africa*
*I've been tryin' to get the mix right*
*But I haven't got it right tonight*

*Ooh, Ooh, Ooh …*

*I've a fifteen year old moustache*
*I'm so desperate for to be a man*
*People tell me to shave it off*
*If I shave it, I'm a boy again*
*Watch my father and my brother*
*Fixing old cars*
*And their rough oil stained hands*
*Are skilled and scarred*

*Ooh, Ooh, Ooh …*

*Behind this big rusty shed door*
*There's a punch bag and a clapped out car*
*As the car sits on breeze blocks*
*The punch bag takes some heavy shots*
*Down the lane way sniffin petrol*
*I thought pebbledash was snow*
*As I stumbled in a blizzard*
*The pain inside me disappeared*
*Cross the city down the alleys*
*A thousand kids like me*
*They are watching through red eyes*
*The flock of little birds gracefully gliding by*

*Ooh, Ooh, Ooh.....*

*Fought in the lane, lost in the lane*
*Swallowed the shame, then I fought again*
*Fought in the lane, cried in the lane*
*Swallowed the pain, then I fought again*
*Fell in the lane, got back up in the lane*
*Died in the lane, and came alive again*

*We are all in the gutter but some of us are looking at the stars*
*We are all in the gutter but some of us are looking at the stars*
*We are all in the gutter but some of us are looking at the stars*
*We are all in the gutter but some of us are looking at the stars.*
*The stars, ooh the stars, the stars.*

## BIOGRAPHY

After finishing his formal education, Damien Dempsey became a pupil of
the Ballyfermot Rock School for two years, where he studied both musical
performance and the practical demands of the music industry. The school

had its own record label, and students who excelled were awarded a release on the label in question – something Damien Dempsey achieved. This, subsequently, led to the release of the EP *The Contender* in 1995.

Damien's first commercial single two years later, 'Dublin Town', soared to No. 18 in the Irish charts. A re-recorded version of the song also featured on his debut album *They Don't Teach this Shit in School*, which was released in 2000 and included the tracks 'Jealousy', 'NYC Paddy', 'Seanchaí', 'I've No Alibi', 'Chillin', 'It's Important' and 'Bad Time Garda'.

Damien's next release, the *Negative Vibes* EP in 2002, saw him collaborate with Sinéad O'Connor on the title track. Their union led to an invitation from Sinéad to support her on her 2002/2003 Irish, UK and European tour.

*Seize the Day* was released May 2003 in Ireland on Clear Records via Sony and entered the Irish charts at No. 5. Amongst the tracks on this album are 'Negative Vibes', 'Ghosts Of Overdoses', 'It's All Good', 'Celtic Tiger', 'Great Gaels Of Ireland' and 'Marching Season Siege'. It went on to achieve double-platinum sales. Released in May 2004 in the UK via IRL Music, the album was awarded CD of the Week in the *Sunday Times* and received enthusiastic reviews in the national and music press. Damien went on to scoop two awards in the 2004 Irish Meteor Awards.

In 2004, Damien toured extensively, headlining his own shows as well as supporting Bob Dylan during the Irish leg of his European tour and making his debut appearances at the Fleadh and Womad.

He continues to make an impact on the Irish musical scene, and his latest album, *Shots*, entered the Irish album charts at No. 1 and achieved platinum status in December 2005.

Damien has also been the subject of a documentary with the broadcasting of *It's All Good: The Damien Dempsey Story* by independent film-maker Dara McCluskey. The film followed Damien's career up to the release of *Seize the Day* and was broadcast on RTÉ and shown at film festivals in Ireland and New York.

*Gemma Hayes*

## Evening Sun

*Written by Gemma Hayes*
*Taken from the album* Night on My Side

I would like to tell you about how I came to write the song 'Evening Sun'. It's a simple little song, not very complicated, which for me is refreshing. In fact, there are so few words to this song that I just repeat the same lines over and over, but for some reason I never get tired of singing it.

Sometimes I fall in love with a song, not because of the song itself but because of what it reminds me of. Sometimes it's a time, sometimes a person. I wrote this song when I was living off Dartmouth Square near Ranelagh, Dublin. At the time, I had moved from Sandymount to be closer to my friend Mic Christopher who will be forever dearly missed. We had struck up a friendship earlier in the year when he handed me a tiny book on how to be 'happy'. He was one of those people that knew and could sense a little more than the average bear. He made me happy and for a while I made him happy too.

It was one of those golden summer afternoons, and Mic, a few other friends and myself went out on the town. We ended up back at Dartmouth Square, sitting on the steps of Mic's house, playing guitar and having lots of fun. It was such a warm, carefree evening where I felt truly happy for a moment. I wanted to hold on to it and to remember it forever. So I wrote 'Evening Sun'.

It was one of those songs that sort of fell out of me. I wanted it to sound lazy and sunburned like the way we were that evening. I guess the song was about being aware of something beautiful but also being aware of the fact that it would leave you soon and there would be nothing you could do about it. I recorded the song soon after I wrote it. I'm so glad I did that because the song was fresh and I meant every word of it. Simple as it was – for me it was powerful.

Well that's it really. There were no fireworks or major traumas around the writing of this song, just a brief but wonderful moment of happiness.

### Evening Sun

*Evening sun*
*Why don't you stay*
*Just a little longer, please*

*My friends and I*
*Well, our party's almost over*
*Why don't you stay*
*Just a little longer please*

*'Cause I need you bad*
*I need you better*
*I need you bad*
*That I could kill*
*I need you bad*
*I need you better*
*Come on*

*Evening sun*
*Why don't you stay*
*Just a little longer, please*

*My friends and I*
*Well, our party's almost over*
*Why don't you stay*
*Just a little longer please*

*'Cause I need you bad*
*I need you better*
*I need you bad*
*That I could kill*
*I need you bad*
*I need you better*
*Come on, now*

## BIOGRAPHY

Twenty-seven-year-old Tipperary native Gemma Hayes has made a huge impact on the music scene since coming to prominence. Her unique style has attracted fans of all ages and has earned her an impressive reputation for one so young.

Following the success of her debut album, *Night On My Side*, which was released in 2002, Gemma found she had a mental block when trying to compose tracks for her second album, and it took her many hours of solitude, and a long time, to find her feet again.

She travelled to the bright lights of LA in search of musicians to work with on her next offering, and there she met and worked with writers and producers of the highest calibre.

It was in LA that Gemma first met drummer Joey Waronker, and this led to her working with the likes of Josh Klinghoffer, Cedric LeMoyne and Roger Manning Jr.

It has been a long and mystical journey, but Gemma is justifiably happy with where she is today and with the production of her second album *The Roads Don't Love You,* which includes the tracks 'Two Step', 'Easy on The Eye', 'Another For The Darkness', 'Tomorrow', 'Happy, Sad' and 'Undercover'.

*Leslie Dowdall*

## Wonderful Thing

*Written by Leslie Dowdall*

*Taken from the album* No Guilt, No Guile

I wrote 'Wonderful Thing' in 1996. It arose out of a lot of different things in my life, one of which was the fact that I had just recovered from an illness and I just felt so joyful to be alive. Sometimes songs take a week or longer to do, but this was just one of those songs that came to me immediately. I wrote it in less than a day, and I remember annoying everybody in my excitement because, though it was really simple, I knew it had something special about it!

It's extraordinary because it is still being played all these years later. It was used in the Lotto adverts on television, and it's one of the most requested songs at people's weddings. It seems to appeal to a lot of people.

For me, I had one particular person in mind at the time I wrote it, but it's one of those songs that can be interpreted in lots of different ways.

It was originally recorded on my *No Guilt, No Guile* album in 1997 and later rereleased in an orchestral piece for the Irish Cancer Society in 1998. It's a very positive and upbeat song and it has been lucky for me.

### Wonderful Thing

You are my
You are my wonderful thing.

Come closer
Stand by me
We shall be free.
Stick by me
Then guide me
And lead me through.
Cos I want and I need to
Be right by your side.

*Chorus*
You are my
You are my wonderful thing.
You are my
You are my wonderful thing.

Can you hear me
Calling out your
Calling out your name.
Can't you see that
I am falling
And I don't know what to say.
Cause you are the brightest star
That I have ever seen.
That finds me
Sets my soul free
This is where I long to be.

*Chorus*
You are my
You are my wonderful thing.
You are my
You are my wonderful thing.

Watch the sun rise
In the big blue
See it shine right through.
I long to embrace you
Can't escape you
Can you feel it too?
Cause you are the brightest star
That I have ever seen.
That guides me
Sets my soul free
Wherever I roam.

## BIOGRAPHY

Though now recognised as one of Ireland's leading singer-songwriters, Leslie Dowdall originally came to everyone's attention in the 1980s via In Tua Nua, as the voice of the band that for seven years fused Celtic traditions with rock. She, however, wanted the space to find her own style, and the band broke up in 1990.

Leslie's solo career then took off in 1997 with the release of her debut album entitled *No Guilt, No Guile*. There were eight original songs on the album and two covers chosen to fit the mood and sound of the entire album. *No Guilt, No Guile* was one of the musical highlights of 1997 and was deemed the best possible introduction to Leslie's solo talent for her fans. She won the 1997 Best Solo Female artist at the Heineken/Hot Press Music Awards.

After the release of *No Guilt, No Guile*, Leslie teamed up with Ronan Hardiman for his debut solo album *Solas*. Towards the end of 1997, Leslie established her own record label, LD Records, under which the appropriately titled single 'Freedom' was released. It was under this label that she released a new set of songs which would ultimately form the album *Out There*, which was released in 1998. This was produced by ex-Fountain Head Pat O'Donnell and was recorded over a twelve-month period in her own studio, based in County Wicklow. Brendan Murphy of The Four of Us co-wrote 'Out There' and '8,000 Miles', and other musicians appearing on the album include Bill Shanley, Trevor Knight, Wayne Sheehy, Tony Molloy, Lloyd Byrne, Jim Sheridan, Steve Belton and Karl Breen. The single releases from this album were 'Freedom', 'Angel' and '8,000 Miles'. *Out There* not only confirmed Leslie's ability as one of Ireland's best female singers but also her natural talent as a songwriter.

In 1999, Leslie featured in a series of Beatles Celebration Concerts at the National Concert Hall. She then renewed her previously successful partnership with Ronan Hardiman and provided vocals for his second solo album *Anthem*, released in 2000. She was also the featured vocalist in the musical production *The Flight of the Earls*, which was composed and written by Mary Ronayne-Keane.

*Mick Hanly*

## Crusader

*Written by Mick Hanly*

*Taken from the album* Wish Me Well

I wrote 'Crusader' after reading about an Australian lady called Robyn Davidson, who set out on a remarkable journey across the Australian desert in the 1980s. She was determined to complete this mission, and she did it alone, apart from a dog and some camels she had trained. She set off from Alice Springs and learned to fend for herself, finding food and doing repairs. It took her six months in total to walk across the desert from Alice Springs to the western coast of Australia.

A fortnight into the journey, she woke one day to find that the camels had gone – with all her food and equipment with them! This was a major setback, and she spoke of how the string holding her soul together began to unravel. I was very taken with that description and decided to write a song about it, changing the phrase a little to 'the silken thread' that 'keeps a hold on you'. I wrote about that particular woman and that particular time in her life.

I wrote about her feelings of uncertainty and fear on this inspirational and extraordinary journey. She now lives in London and has written a book about her experiences entitled *Tracks*.

It is a very special song to me as well because it is the first song I ever wrote that was recorded by another artist.

## Crusader

*There's a wilderness*
*It's a no-man's land*
*Between Alice Springs and the ocean*
*Seventeen hundred miles of burning sand*
*And a silken thread keeps a hold on you*
*When the emptiness like a potion tends to fray your reason strand by strand*
*And there's no more need for the mask you wear*
*When the last goodbyes have been said*
*So kiss the cheeks of you dearest friends*
*And turn to the desert ahead*
*Now you're on your own like a sailing ship*
*You're the captain, crew and sailors*
*Turn around and this is what you see*

### Chorus
*This me facing me all alone*
*'Cause I choose to be with the wind and the sun on me only me*

*Now you dream so much about being lost*
*Your ghost by a coolebah sleeping*
*Haunts you and whispers in your ear*
*Give up give up this lonely road*
*No one knows the promise you're keeping*
*You can't touch the emptiness out here*
*But the grace that mends this broken wing*

*The blue sky to regain*
*Will lift those feet and raise those eyes*
*To face the desert again*
*As the dawn reveals the journey's end*
*In truth it's only beginning*
*And it's as big as your eyes wish to see*

**Chorus**
*This me facing me all alone*
*'Cause I choose to be with the wind and the sun on me only me*

# BIOGRAPHY

Mick Hanly has undergone a series of transitions in his musical journey – from would-be teenage rock 'n' roller to professional folk singer to country singer and, more significantly, country songwriter of world-class stature. He has earned himself an international reputation and the respect of both peers and listeners alike.

The arrival in his home town of Limerick of rock 'n' roll in the mid-1950s, and the influence of Elvis, Buddy Holly and the Everly Brothers, fired Mick's imagination and led to the purchase of his first guitar (albeit a toy one) for £2 in Todds of Limerick.

With the 1960s came The Beatles and the beat boom, closely followed by The Beach Boys, The Animals, The Hollies, The Spencer Davis Group and, of course, the weekly local dance-hops – many of which provided the inspiration for the 1980s song 'All I Remember'.

With the completion of his formal education, the young Mick was expected to find a 'real job' and, in 1970, started work with the Electricity Supply Board. However, he continued to nurture his love of music and found himself stirred by the tunes of Sean Ó Riada and legendary Clare uilleann piper Willie Clancy.

The traditional sounds of Ó Riada and Clancy tugged at his heart in a way that forced him to fully understand his sense of 'Irishness'.

Mick's 'conversion' to traditional Irish music song was assisted by Mícheál Ó Domhnaill. Mick and Mícheál's union led to the formation of Monroe, who went on to secure a spot as support for Planxty's Irish Tour in 1973. They released an album, *Folk Weave*, but parted company in 1975 when Mícheál went on to join The Bothy Band and Mick headed for France.

Back home again in the late 1970s, Mick recorded 'A Kiss In The Morning Early' and 'As I Went Over Blackwater' with some of Ireland's most-revered musicians, including Dónal Lunny, Andy Irvine, Matt Molloy, Paddy Glackin, Noel Hill, Peter Brown and Declan Sinnott.

Following a brief stint in Moving Hearts, Mick again embarked on a solo journey and penned songs, such as 'Open Those Gates' and 'Sorry I Said What I Said'.

Then 1989 saw the release of a Mary Black album on which she covered what was to become Mick's most famous song 'Past The Point Of Rescue'. This was soon snapped up by Nashville country producer Jim Rooney, who subsequently passed the song to Hal Ketchum, and the rest, as they say, is history.

His latest album *Wish Me Well* includes the tracks 'Dust In The Storm', 'I Feel I Should Be Calling You', 'Damaged Halo', 'Too Old For Fairytales', 'Trying To Get To St Nazaire', 'I Am, I Am', 'Crusader', 'Wish Me Well', 'Cold, Cold, World', 'Shellakabookee Boy' and 'When Nobody's Beating On The Drums'.

*Roesy*

## Home It Has Flown

*Written by Roesy*

*Taken from the album* Colour Me Colourful

The song I would choose is 'Home It Has Flown', which was, for me, different to my usual type of writing. It came about after I had been to the Museum for Aboriginal Arts and Culture in Melbourne when I was living in Australia one year. It is about the lost generation of Aborigines and one certain aspect of their lives.

The song comes from the story of a young girl who was put on a train by her parents to embark on a journey, to be met at the other end by an aunt. Somehow, she died while on the trip, and the unbelievable thing was that the people in charge, or the authorities, just took her body and buried her in the middle of nowhere. They didn't even inform her family – that was the inhumane way in which those people were treated.

Another story from the museum was about how Aboriginal children who have died are also segregated in graveyards and treated in a hostile way.

There was a story of a gardener who had a lot of compassion for these children, probably because he had seen so many deaths. He went out of his way to recognise them and acknowledge their lives and their death by planting irises on their graves.

'Home It Has Flown' was written because of those two stories and also because of the death of my friend's mother. It's written in the hope that there is something better out there, that there is another life and that somewhere, people don't treat others in this way.

### Home It Has Flown

*Up the dawn it comes rising*
*East in the arms of loved ones*
*Watch as the light to the west runs*
*Home it has flown*

*Pinched the violet clover*
*Sweet taste in the cool rain*
*Silence flown with the lone crane*
*Home it has flown*

*Wise and unfallen stars*
*Colour your mind*
*Wise and unfallen stars*
*Would never leave you behind*

*Time so fast blazing*
*Trails from day into nightshade*
*What of the castles our hands made*
*Home it has flown*

*When the iris hits the grave*
*Memories deep underground now*

*Home the soul has flown*
*Home it has flown*

*Wise and unfallen stars*
*Colour your mind*
*Wise and unfallen stars*
*Would never leave you behind*

*Up the dawn come rising*
*East in the arms of loved ones*
*Watch as the light to the west runs*
*Home it has flown*
*Home it has flown*
*Home it has flown*

## BIOGRAPHY

Offaly-born Roesy was destined to have a musical career, having been heavily influenced by his father who had a keen musical interest. From listening to his father's records, Roesy progressed to writing his own lyrics and teaching himself to play the guitar.

His desire to travel further afield was to form the inspiration for many of his songs, and his wanderlust had a lasting impact on his music.

Through his career, he has shared the stage with Bert Jansch, Ron Sexsmith, Paul Brady, Billy Bragg, John Martyn, Davy Spillane, Donovan, Shane MacGowan and celebrated Irish poet Paul Durcan.

Roesy featured in the first *Other Voices* television series on RTÉ. He was nominated for Best New Irish Act in the 2004 Meteor Music Awards and voted No. 8 in the trad/folk section of the Annual Hot Press Awards 2005. His song 'Potosi Mine' was included in the *Diamond Mountain Session Presents* compilation CD, which also featured Sinéad O'Connor, Steve Earle, Natalie Merchant and Sharon Shannon.

Roesy is also a talented artist and designed the mural used as the backdrop to the photo shoot for the album sleeve. From early childhood, art has been a part of his life, and he studied Fine Art and Design at Galway's Regional Technical College. After eight years of focusing solely on his music career, he returned to painting and, in November 2003, had a solo sell-out show at The Cross Gallery, Dublin. He was part of Tone, a group show at The Roundstone and Galway arts festivals 2004. He enjoyed another solo sell-out show at The Wexford Opera Festival in 2004 and was involved in an art exhibition and auction at James Adam Fine Art Auctioneers, Dublin. He has also exhibited in Denmark and Australia and featured as part of Art in the West in Galway last year. His work was on display for much of this year at The Roundstone Arts Centre, Connemara.

Roesy's newest album *Colour Me Colourful*, produced by Ken McHugh, was released in May 2006.

Phil Skelly

*Sonny Condell*

## Down In The City

*Written by Sonny Condell*

*Taken from the album* Camouflage

I suppose my most well-known song would be 'Down In The City', first released on my solo album, *Camouflage*, in 1977. I wrote it after a trip to California. I was looking out at the low hills in California and I took a photograph through the back window of the car in which I was travelling.

Some time later, I was back in the UK, travelling from London to Glasgow. One time, I was just sitting on the side of a stage when the same photograph came into my head, and I just wrote the song there and then. It's really about going from one big city to another and about the changes that entails. It's a little vague, but it's about the new things that come your way, the settling in and new challenges and the people that you meet. It's a song that the audiences love, and we always make sure to include it either at the start or at the end of a gig.

## Down In The City

*You're out in the night so blue*
*you summer star.*
*I'm down on the road of speed*
*a steady drive.*
*I'm ending my day with you*
*so hold me close.*
*I trust you will lay me down*
*when time is up.*

*Chorus*
*I'm down in the city*
*you know where to find me.*
*I'm down in the city*
*you know where to find me.*
*I'm up on the top floor*
*I'm up on the top floor*
*just under the moon.*

*And heaven is very blue*
*this summer day.*
*I'm rolling my window down*
*to hear the sea.*
*I'm fading from someones view*
*into the hills.*
*I trust you will lay me down*
*when time is up.*

*Chorus*
*I'm down in the city*
*you know where to find me.*
*I'm down in the city*
*you know where to find me.*
*I'm up on the top floor*

*I'm up on the top floor*
*just under the moon.*

*I'm talking to the great pole star*
*he looks down notes down each word I say*
*and we all live a lot*
*we all*
*give a bit*
*we all*
*think a lot*
*too much*
*too much*

**Chorus**
*I'm down in the city*
*you know where to find me.*
*I'm down in the city*
*you know where to find me.*
*I'm up on the top froor*
*I'm up on the top floor*
*just under the moon.*

*You're out in the night so blue*
*you summer star.*
*I'm down on the road of speed*
*a steady drive.*
*I'm fading from someones view*
*into the hills.*
*I trust you will lay me down*
*when time is up*
*when time is up*
*when time is up.*

# BIOGRAPHY

A native of County Wicklow, Sonny Condell has been an integral part of the Irish music scene since the early 1970s and is perhaps best known for his innovative collaborations with Leo O'Kelly in Tír na nÓg and with Philip King in Scullion.

Ironically, for all their success, Tír na nÓg came about quite accidentally when the musically mismatched Sonny Condell and Leo O'Kelly joined forces back in the early 1970s. Leo had been working in a mixture of various bands and showbands (playing everything from Clancy Brothers songs to the Monkees and Tom Jones covers) when he stumbled across Sonny and his cousin, who had been performing together. Leo had already toured Britain and Europe with Dónal Lunny, during a brief spell with Emmet Spiceland, and this only served to fuel his desire to try and make it as a singer-songwriter.

Sonny, it soon transpired, harboured similar ambitions, and together they fuelled their passion for songwriting. They hit the bright lights of London and, in just two days, Tír na nÓg had secured a recording deal with Chrysalis Records and started touring the pubs and clubs of England. They produced three albums between 1971 and 1974 before the duo reluctantly went their separate ways.

It was soon after the split of Tír na nÓg that Sonny recorded *Camouflage*, his first solo album, which features 'Down In The City', 'Camouflage', 'Moondust', 'Red Sail', 'Movie To You', 'Why Do We Fight?', 'Leaders Of Men' and 'Backwaterawhile'. It was released to great critical acclaim and indeed some of the songs were to form the basis for Sonny's next venture in musical collaboration.

Scullion came about in the late 1970s, through a chance meeting between Philip King and Sonny Condell. Sonny was finding his new musical path after the break up of Tír na nÓg, and Philip was also looking for a new start. Assisted by Greg Boland on guitar and Jimmy O'Brien Moran on pipes, the band started rehearsing in a small apartment above a chip shop in Dún Laoghaire, County Dublin. Mulligan Records, who had already worked with Sonny on *Camouflage*, offered Scullion a recording contract, and they found themselves developing a fan base and touring the world. They recorded three albums: *Balance and Control*, *White Side of Night* and *Spin*.

During the late 1980s, the band went into semi-retirement, occasionally playing one-off concerts, while Sonny concentrated on pursuing his solo career. In 2001, they reformed to re-record 'Eyelids Into Snow' for use in a television advert. They also recorded a new version of 'Down In The City'.

While both Tír na nÓg and Scullion continue to play live concerts, Sonny's primary creative outlet in recent times has been through his solo work, albeit often in collaboration with his band. His solo offerings to date include four albums – *Camouflage*, *Someone to Dance With*, *French Windows* and *Backwaterawhile* – and a fifth is in production.

These days, The Sonny Condell Band has changed its name to Radar. With Sonny's songs providing most of the material, the remaining band members bring their unique mix of jazz, rock and orchestral backgrounds to the table. Joining Sonny in the band are Paul Barrett, Garvan Gallagher, Mick de Hoog and Eddie McGinn. Their new album is called *Navigation*.

*Colin Devlin — The Devlins*

## Waves

*Written by Colin Devlin*

*Taken from the album* Waves

'Waves' is a song I wrote about three years ago and it's the title track on our latest album. It's a kind of feel-good song that I find cheers me up when I'm feeling blue. The lines are simple, 'You beat these things, you ride these waves / Someday soon our luck will change.' They're about the simple everyday things in life. It's about a lot of personal stuff, and it's a song that we've always enjoyed playing, and it's always been well received by the crowd at gigs.

Most of all, it's a song from the heart. A kind of messed-up love song!

## Waves

*I like the way you look at me*
*'Cause nothing here is guaranteed*
*Work so hard to get paid*
*Here alone it feels OK*

*You beat these things, you ride these waves*
*Some day soon our luck will change*
*You beat these things, ride these waves*
*Some day soon our luck will change*

*I don't know where I belong*
*Can't stay down got to move on*
*You give me strength to defeat*
*The steel in my soul, steel on the streets*

*Beneath the concrete lies the beach*
*In my hands not out of reach*

*You beat these things, you ride these waves*
*Some day soon our luck will change*
*Ride these waves*

*Days add up, life goes on*
*Rent comes due, spring comes fall*
*I take you out, I dance with you*
*And fade to black from neon blue*
*Somewhere in the dead of night*
*Our memories remain in light*

*You beat these things, you ride these waves*
*Some day soon our luck will change*

*Ride these waves*
*Ride these waves*

*Our luck is going to change*
*Luck is going to change…*

## BIOGRAPHY

Dublin-born brothers Colin and Peter Devlin continue to musically gel together to provide the perfect ingredients for those blue, blue days, with 'Waves' just one of many feel-good songs produced by this talented twosome.

Their 1993 debut album, *Drift*, was produced by Daniel Lanois and made a lasting impression on their early fan base with tracks such as 'I Knew That', 'Every Time You Go', 'Turn You Round', 'Drift', 'Almost Made You Smile', 'Alone In The Dark' and 'Someone To Talk To'.

This was followed four years later by the album *Waiting*, which included 'World Outside', 'Heaven's Wall', 'Years Could Go By', 'Where Are You Tonight?' and 'Disappear', which achieved gold status and saw them earn their right as one of Ireland's most promising acts.

A move to Kinsale, County Cork, in early 1999 saw the duo set up their own studio and record their third album *Consent*, featuring 'In Seville', 'Snowbirds', 'Montreal' and 'Metro'. This was the lads' first solo attempt at producing and engineering their own work and was clearly a risk worth taking.

Three years later, the brothers sought the expertise of engineer Danton Supple (Coldplay, Doves, Starsailor) for their most adventurous material yet. So came *Waves* in January 2005, which featured the tracks 'Everything Comes Around', 'Sunrise', 'Careless Love', 'Someday', 'Lazarus', 'Don't Let It Break Your Heart', 'Feel It When You're Gone', 'Coming Alive', 'Headstrong' and 'Waves'. Always compelling and emotive, the lyrics emerge from the heart and transport the listener on an unforgettable musical journey.

The Devlins' music has now progressed into film and television: 'Waiting' was included on the *Six Feet Under* soundtrack while 'World Outside' featured in the 2004 film *Closer*.

*Tommy Sands*

## The Music Of Healing

*Written by Tommy Sands and Pete Seeger*
*Taken from the album* The Heart's a Wonder

Pete Seeger and his wife Toshi live in a physically modest, but inspirationally palatial, log cabin in a forest overlooking the Hudson River.

The father of American folk music is over eighty years of age now, but you couldn't define him as old – in many ways, he is one of the youngest people I know. He never stops listening and he never stops learning. With habits like that, it is very difficult to grow old no matter how hard you try.

Pete sings at breakfast, when chopping logs, when washing dishes and at his supper, and you can't help but sing along. Often when we are singing old songs, we are thinking about new ones. 'Do you know a song about eating toast?' asked Pete one morning as he placed a slice of bread in the toaster.

'No,' I replied.

'Well, let's compose one then,' he said.

We made up silly verses and laughed our way through breakfast with Pete's grandson Tao tickling a five-string banjo in accompaniment. Toshi looked up from time to time and shook her head as if to say, 'Crazy as ever, you folk singers,' but deep down she was enjoying it all. Toshi, a wonderful woman, an inspiration to Pete and a kind of mother to us all.

'Why don't you write a song about healing those wounds in your country?' she suggested. 'Yes,' agreed Pete. 'It's amazing how music can help to heal wounds between people and within people.'

'Somebody should write a song about that,' I said, looking at Pete.

'You write it,' he scolded gently.

Some months later, I was back in the USA again. I had written 'The Music Of Healing', and I sang it to Pete, who listened intently. Then he stood up and declared quietly as he viewed the Hudson below, 'It needs another verse.'

'You write it,' I said with a smile.

'My father told me once, many years ago, that truth is like a rabbit in a briar patch, you know that it's there, but you can't catch it. I have always wanted to put that in a song,' he said. 'And my father used to say, "The more you learn, the more you know, the less you knew," ' I laughed.

'But isn't it wonderful to learn,' said Pete, 'even if, and especially if, learning makes you realise you were wrong?'

I knew there were two songs in his musings, but it was only one verse we needed – and we had it already.

*Sometimes the truth's like a hare in the cornfield,*
*You know that it's there but you can't put your arms round it.*
*All we can hope for is to follow its footsteps,*
*Sing me the music of healing.*
*Who would have thought I could feel so contented,*
*To learn I was wrong after all of my rambles?*
*I've learned to be hard and I've learned how to tremble,*
*Sing me the music of healing.*

When I got back home, I went into the studio with Arty McGlynn and began to record the song. Pete would sing his verse in Greenwich Village, supported by his talented grandson Tao, Lisa Gutkin and Greg Anderson, and the tape would be 'flown' into the studio mix in the village of Rostrevor.

> *Ah the heart's a wonder,*
> *Stronger than the guns of thunder,*
> *Even when we're torn asunder,*
> *Love will come again.*

The world was badly in need of healing. Television was bringing the tragedies of Sarajevo into our homes. Then Vedran Smailovic, a gifted cellist, appeared dramatically in the midst of the horrors.

I wanted to include him on our recording, but I had no idea how to track him down. Then Peter Emerson telephoned. He had met Smailovic in Sarajevo on one of his bicycle journeys. Peter was launching his new book *Consensus Politics* in the Mansion House in Dublin. He had written it when he returned from Moscow and he wanted me to sing 'The Music Of Healing' at the function. He asked if I knew a cellist who could play Smailovic's music.

'Could we find the man himself?' I asked.

Several days later, after many phone calls, I drove to Belfast International Airport to await the arrival of a flight from London.

The only son of Yugoslav composer Avdo Smailovic, Vedran had been regarded as something of a young musical messiah, receiving a special award as a child from President Tito. He would become the principal cellist in the Sarajevo Opera orchestra. When the war began, his theatre was destroyed by a bomb, and, on 27 May 1992, twenty-two of his neighbours were killed as they stood queuing for bread. For twenty-two days, each day marking the death of each neighbour who had died, Smailovic went out onto the street, dressed in evening suit and bow tie and sat down to play 'Albinoni's Adagio'. A CNN reporter ran up to him, complete with camera and flak jacket, and shouted, 'Mr Smailovic, are you not crazy for playing your cello while they're shelling Sarajevo?' Smailovic looked at him, more in sadness than in anger. 'You ask me if I am crazy for playing my cello while they shell Sarajevo,' he said, 'but you don't ask if they are not crazy for shelling Sarajevo while I play my cello.'

Vedran arrived at Belfast airport without his cello. It had disappeared in the rubble of war. We quickly set about the task of borrowing an instrument for him.

'The Music Of Healing', with Pete's voice and Vedran's cello, became the opening track on a *The Heart's a Wonder*. John Hume launched the CD at an event organised by Kevin McCaul in Derry's Calgach Centre and declared 'The Music Of Healing' a new anthem for our times.

At the Fiddler's Green Festival in Rostrevor in 1995 we decided to let 'The Music Of Healing' flow into a seminar. We invited a few musicians to create an atmosphere of humanity and neighbourliness and two politicians from opposing sides to talk about the common ground we all shared. The two politicians were Francie Molloy from Sinn Féin, the political wing of the IRA, and Belfast Unionist Roy Garland, who had links with loyalist paramilitary groups. Their talk was forthright and straight, of what was on their mind and on their party line, but they talked. We met in Harmony Hall in Rostrevor and I asked my good friend and neighbour Mary McAleese to chair the discussion.

Mary was a brilliant lecturer in law at Queen's University. She knew the issues at stake in Northern Irish politics and was very supportive of community events in Rostrevor. On one occasion, local playwright Síobhán Farrell Ó Dubháin cast Mary and myself as long-lost lovers in a play she was putting on in the local hall. I played the Rat Catcher and Mary was the Sanitary Inspector. Mary, however, was preparing for another role in real life. She was elected President of Ireland in 1997 and took up residence in Áras an Uachtaráin in Dublin's Phoenix Park. She would go on to make 'bridge-building' her presidential theme. She invited me to present a number of 'Music of Healing' events, featuring Irish uilleann pipes and Orange Lambeg drums.

## The Music Of Healing

*Don't beat the drum to frighten the children,*
*Don't sing the songs about winning and losing,*
*Sit down beside me the green fields are bleeding,*

Sing me the music of healing.
Sing me a song of a lover returning,
The darker the night the nearer the morning
Sing me the news of a new day that's dawning
Sing me the music of healing.

Ah the heart's a wonder, stronger than the guns of thunder
Even when we're torn asunder,
Love will come again

Sometimes the truth's like a hare in the cornfield,
You know that it's there but you can't put your arms round it.
All we can hope for is to follow its footsteps,
Sing me the music of healing.
Who would have thought I could feel so contented
To learn I was wrong after all of my rambles?
I've learned to be hard and I've learned how to tremble,
Sing me the music of healing.

Somehow the cycle of vengeance keeps turning,
'Til each other's sorrows and songs we start learning.
Peace is the prize for those who are daring,
Sing me the music of healing.
Time is your friend it cures all your sorrows,
But how can I wait on another tomorrow?
One step today and another will follow,
Sing me the music of healing.

## BIOGRAPHY

From his pioneering days with the highly influential Sands Family, bringing
Irish music from New York's Carnegie Hall to Moscow's Olympic Stadium,

Tommy Sands has developed into one of the most powerful songwriters and enchanting solo performers in Ireland today.

His songwriting, which draws the admiration of Nobel Poet Laureate Seamus Heaney and father of folk music Pete Seeger, has seen his material recorded by respected artists such as Joan Baez, Kathy Mattea, Dolores Keane, Seán Keane, Frank Patterson, Dick Gaughan and The Dubliners.

His albums with the Sands Family include *First Day and the Second Day*, *The Third Day*, *As I Roved Out*, *Winds of Freedom*, *Now and Then*, *Sands Family at Home*, *Tell Me What You See*, *Real Irish Folk* and *The Sands Family Collection*, while his solo albums include *To Shorten the Winter*, *The Heart's a Wonder*, *Beyond the Shadows*, *Hedges of County Down*, *Down by Bendy's Lane*, *Singing of the Times* and *Folk from the Mournes*.

Though regularly performing all around the world, Tommy enjoys bringing his music to more intimate surroundings. One of his current projects is teaching prisoners in Reno, Nevada, to write their own songs with which to defend themselves in court. This unique project is currently creating a stir in the world of community art in the USA while, back home in Northern Ireland, he has just completed a CD written with Protestant and Catholic schoolchildren about their own areas in towns and villages around Northern Ireland.

In May 2002, Tommy Sands received an honourary doctorate of Letters from the University of Nevada for his outstanding work as a musician and as an ambassador for peace and understanding, and Reno pronounced 18 May as Tommy Sands Day.

In December 2002, although the Northern Ireland Assembly had been stood down, Sands managed to persuade the members to return for a special Christmas musical party together. The concert, which was recorded for the Sands weekly radio programme, later received a special award at the World Festival of TV and Radio in New York. In 2005, Tommy published his book *The Songman*.

Cathal Dawson

*Nina Hynes*

## Systematically

*Written by Nina Hynes and Derek Cosgrave*

*Yet to be released*

In this song, I get to be a malfunctioning sexy robot who is dark in nature but brings hope, fun and joy.

I wrote the lyrics for this song in 2006. I wrote the music with a fellow robot called Derek Cosgrave.

It allows me to see beyond the confines of my emotional window. It allows me to be bold, sexy, dark and hopeful. I wanted to make music with an interesting angle, which people can dance to in an uninhibited fashion.

The song hasn't been released as yet. It is a side project and we are trying to think of a bad name. It's kind of dirty synth robotic suicide pop music.

## Systematically

*Systematically, fixing all of me.*
*I'm a new machine, I'm becoming clean.*
*Mechanically, fix my memory.*
*I won't procrastinate, what is now is great.*
*Some symmetry, oooooh, like plastic surgery,*
*It's biblical, ah, and it's a physical urgency.*

*This should last for all,*
*This should last for ever and ever.*
*This should last for all, this should last for ever and ever.*
*Say what you need, what you need, what you need,*
*Say what you need, what you need, what you need.*

*So brutally, we can love and leave.*
*Show me how to feel, can you make me real.*
*We fascinate, become obsolete and we radiate,*
*Just so that we can meet.*
*We need belief, ooooh, we need some binary.*
*It's biblical, ah, and it's a physical urgency.*

*This should last for all.*
*This should last for ever and ever.*
*This should last for all, this should last for ever and ever.*
*Say what you mean, what you mean, what you mean.*
*Say what you mean, what you mean.*
*Miaow.*
*Ah ah ah ah ah ah ah...oh oh oh oh oh...ah ah ah ah ah*
*...oh oh oh oh oh...*

# BIOGRAPHY

Nina Hynes has been playing with recorded sound since she was seven, when she used to collect the tapes of bleeps from the heart machines in the hospital where her aunt worked. She used to record herself singing over the bleeps.

She began to play the piano around this time also and wrote her first song when she was eight, which was about a man who used to dress up as a woman, called 'Big Woman'. Since then, she has learned the guitar, and her solo shows often incorporate live layering and sampling using guitar pedals, spoons and whatever is at hand.

She writes songs and music on guitar, piano, harp, computer or whatever instrument is lying around. She tours mostly solo but has been involved in many bands – instrumental, experimental, acoustic, electronic and electro rock. Often, her shows are atmospheric, using costumes and visuals edited live to the music.

Her first solo release *Creation* (mini-album) was released in 1999, and her subsequent debut album *Staros* was released in 2002. Both are critically acclaimed in Ireland and the USA (where she has toured extensively). Amazon.com voted *Creation* No. 44 in their Top 100 Releases of the Year.

In 2003, she was nominated as Best Female in the Meteor Awards. She has performed on over twenty compilations, soundtracks and releases and has collaborated with many people, including the experimental French composer Hector Zazou, Brian Eno and Harold Budd. Actress and singer Jane Birkin ('Je T'Aime') has recently covered a song of Nina's on a collaboration album with Hector Zazou.

She released a hand-made limited edition EPS on her own label Transplant Records and, in the past two years, has begun touring solo around Europe. She is currently working on two albums and an EP and is at college studying sound engineering and music technology.

Her song 'Universal' made the final fifty in the International Songwriting Competition, the biggest and most prestigious songwriting competition in the USA.

# Sources of Love

Phil Coulter

## The Town I Loved So Well

*Written by Phil Coulter*

*Taken from the album* The Songs I Love So Well

My choice is between 'The Town I Loved So Well' and 'Scorn Not His Simplicity', but I think I will have to go for 'The Town I Loved So Well'. I wrote it back in 1970. I had been on one of my regular visits home to Derry and had seen so many changes. I could see just how big the fallout from The Troubles was. It was affecting my hometown; there were physical scars on the landscape checkpoints and barbed wire. There were armoured patrols cruising down the streets, helicopters hovering around and the people of Derry had no choice but to get used to it. It was something you noticed a lot more after being away. Equally as depressing was the effect on the whole emotional landscape. Derry used to be a city of music and fun and now it was a depressed area. It was an unemployment black spot – women went to work and the men stayed at home and looked after the house and the children. The Derry people went from being a carefree community to having an air of resignation about them. They no longer had a skip in their step; they stayed off the streets at night and there was a gloom in the air.

It had a traumatic impact on me. The images never left me, Derry never left me, no matter where I was in the world. It was also a time when there was internment. I knew at first-hand people I had grown up with, people whose only crime, in the eyes of police intelligence, was to be a member of the GAA, or to attend *céilís* – anything remotely Gaelic equalled republicanism. Men were dragged out of their beds for no good reason, leaving wives and children in bits. It was a total invasion and rape of Derry City.

In response to this, I wrote a song called 'Free the People' and, looking back, it was written in haste and it was a knee-jerk reaction to what was going on. The song was very ill thought out. It was simply an instant and angry reaction to what had happened. It was something I had to get out of my system.

Parallel to this, I was working with The Dubliners. The much-lamented Luke Kelly and I were great friends. Luke had an encyclopedic knowledge of folk music. He had very strong political views and cared passionately about everything. I learned an awful lot from him. He was always asking me to write a different type of song, one that was cut from a different cloth than the pop ones I had become known for, such as 'Puppet On A String' and 'Congratulations', and Luke badgered me until I did.

When my first son was born with Down's Syndrome, I wrote 'Scorn Not His Simplicity', and it was as far away from a commercial pop song as it could be. It deeply affected me because I was peeling off layers of myself and I was not particularly comfortable about that. But that song broke the log jam, and I found that I could think about writing songs about important subjects and tackle real issues.

At this time, the Troubles in Derry had left me so moved and so traumatised and frustrated that, in a way, it was inevitable that I would write something about what was going on. I was determined that this time I would get it right, and I wanted to think it through completely. I had the music to the song in a matter of days, but the lyrics took months because I was aware that the words I used could add to the volatility of the situation and add fuel to the flame, and I didn't want to write just another rebel song. 'The Town

I Loved So Well' has often been referred to as a love song. It is about my love of Derry and my sadness at its change, but it is a song that has been interpreted for many other cities around the world.

Writing the song was painstaking and challenging, but I felt it was important that what was happening should be chronicled in a song and, as I'm from Derry, I understood exactly what needed to be said. I had grown up there and I understood the complexities of the situation. Now, over thirty years later, the song has reached anthemic proportions. It was initially a very specific song because it identifies certain roads and streets, and it was very personal to people living in Derry, but to see it as just about Derry would be to ignore the power of the song.

A few years back, a BBC documentary showed footage of a famous Japanese singer and fifty of her followers who, on a visit to Ireland, paid a visit to the Bogside and sang 'The Town I Loved so Well' in Japanese. That was a very proud moment for me and reinforced what I believe about the song. When I was 'giving birth' to the song, I was aware that though it originated in Derry, it could apply to any volatile situation in any country, and it has now been translated into many different languages.

For many years, 'Danny Boy' was sung by Derry fans at important matches. One year, I went to Croke Park to see Derry play Cork in the All-Ireland final and to hear both sets of fans sing 'The Town I Loved So Well' was the most hair-raising experience. I've also performed it for former US President Bill Clinton in the White House, and it's been recorded numerous times.

Around the time of the millennium, there was an RTÉ poll for the Top 100 songs. No. 1 was 'White Christmas', No. 2 was 'My Way' and No. 3 was 'The Town I Loved So Well'. The importance of that song for me cannot be quantified in dollars and cents. If you look at all my songs purely on a income level that song wouldn't even be in league division one, but it's still probably the most important song I've ever written.

It will always be my favourite song.

## The Town I Loved So Well

*In my memory I will always see*
*the town that I have loved so well,*
*Where our school played ball by the Gas Yard wall*
*and we laughed through the smoke and the smell*
*Going home in the rain, running up the Dark Lane*
*past the Jail and down behind the fountain*
*Those were happy days in so many, many ways*
*in the town I loved so well*

*In the early morning the shirt factory horn*
*called women from Creggan, the Moor and the Bog*
*While the men on the dole played a mother's role,*
*fed the children and then walked the dog*
*And when times got tough there was just about enough*
*But they saw it through without complaining,*
*For deep inside was a burning pride*
*in the town I loved so well.*

*There was music there in the Derry air*
*like a language that we all could understand*
*I remember the day that I earned my first pay*
*When I played in a small pick-up band*
*There I spent my youth and to tell you the truth*
*I was sad to leave it all behind me*
*For I learned about life and I'd found a wife*
*in the town I loved so well*

*But when I've returned how my eyes have burned*
*to see how a town could be brought to its knees*
*By the armoured cars and the bombed-out bars*
*and the gas that hangs on to every breeze*
*Now the army's installed by that old gas yard wall*

*and the damned barbed wire gets higher and higher*
*With their tanks and their guns, oh my God, what have they done*
*to the town I loved so well*

*Now the music's gone but they carry on*
*for their spirit's been bruised, never broken*
*They will not forget but their hearts are set*
*on tomorrow and peace once again*
*For what's done is done and what's won is won*
*and what's lost is lost and gone forever*
*I can only pray for a bright, brand new day*
*in the town I loved so well*

## BIOGRAPHY

One in a family of five, Phil was born in Derry in, as he says himself, 'an era of air-raid shelters and ration books'. It was, he recalls, a happy and carefree household where music was celebrated. His father was from Strangford in County Down and played the fiddle ,and his mother, who was from the Markets in Belfast, played the piano and they enjoyed every note.

The young Phil was a pupil of St Columb's in Derry before entering Queen's University, Belfast, to study music. He travelled to London in 1964 to pursue fame and fortune – and got both! Just a few short years later, he was working with everyone from Van Morrison to Tom Jones to Jerry Lee Lewis and The Rolling Stones. Then came his first major success: 'Puppet On A String', which won the Eurovision Song Contest for the UK in 1967. It went on to be a huge international hit, clocking up over 100 different versions. The next year, the same winning formula fell short by just one point as Cliff Richard sang Phil's 'Congratulations' in the 1968 contest. Those two songs alone sold over 10 million records!

Coulter's friendship with actor Richard Harris led the duo to record a song together, and so 'My Boy' was born, which two years later became an international smash hit for none other than Elvis Presley.

As the 1970s beckoned, pop became the way to go, and it was during the 1970s that Phil wrote many hit songs for The Bay City Rollers, including 'Remember', 'Shang-a-Lang', 'Summer Love Sensation' and 'All Of Me Loves All Of You'. It was also during this time that he wrote 'The Town I Loved So Well'.

However, despite the bright lights of London, Phil was steadfastly, dearly holding on to his Irish roots. In the early 1970s, he produced three ground-breaking albums with Planxty (Liam O'Flynn, Dónal Lunny, Andy Irvine and Christy Moore) and went on to produce with The Dubliners and The Furey Brothers.

In 1984, Phil fulfilled a personal ambition when he recorded an instru-mental album entitled *Classic Tranquility*. This was to be a momentous move – the album became one of the biggest-selling albums ever in Ireland. *Sea of Tranquility* followed and surpassed the success of *Classic Tranquility*.

Phil Coulter has performed at Carnegie Hall, the White House and St Patrick's Cathedral, New York. He has played live outdoors to a crowd of 600,000 on Capitol Hill in Washington, DC, with the National Symphony Orchestra, and also marched at the head of the St Patrick's Day Parade in New York with former Mayor Giuliani.

He has presented three series of his own television programme for RTÉ, *Coulter and Company*, through which he has met and performed with some of today's best-known musicians.

The star of the town he loved so well continues to rise.

*Honor Heffernan*

## A Time For Love

*Written by Johnny Mandel and Paul Francis Webster*

*Taken from the album* Fire and Ice

There are probably hundreds of songs that I could choose, but this one popped into my head instantly.

It's a very philosophical song. It's about the various things we go through, as babies and children and then as teenagers. It's about growing older, and it points out that through all of those times, through all of those experiences, there's always a time for love, and it's just a song that I think has beautiful, beautiful lyrics.

I only really heard 'A Time For Love' a couple of years ago, but it would probably be the kind of song that would run through my mind, and it represents the way I feel about life. It's a lot like the way I see music and communicating. I suppose when you are listening to music you don't really think about what age you are music is ageless in that way.

I recorded 'A Time For Love' on *Fire and Ice*, an album I released in October

2005, and I've been touring with it since, so I've been performing the song live and the audiences have been responding really well to it. It's a very, very powerful song and states quite simply that 'love is all', and it says that in the context of an individual life.

## A Time For Love

*A time for summer skies*
*For hummingbirds and butterflies*
*And tender words that harmonise with love*

*A time for climbing hills*
*For leaning out of windowsills*
*Admiring daffodils above*

*A time for holding hands together*
*A time for rainbow coloured weather*
*A time of make believe that we've been dreaming of*

*As time goes drifting by*
*The willow bends and so do I*
*But oh my love whatever skies above*
*I've known a time for spring*
*A time for fall*
*But best of all*
*A time for love*

*A time for holding hands together*
*A time for rainbow-coloured weather*
*A time of make believe that we've been dreaming of*

*As time goes drifting by*
*The willow bends and so do I*
*But oh my love whatever skies above*
*I've known a time for spring*
*A time for fall*
*But best of all*
*A time for love*

## BIOGRAPHY

It's been an incredible three decades since Honor Heffernan first came to prominence as a singer and an actress, and in that time she has been both critically and publicly acclaimed as someone with the unique ability to shine through many genres of music, from jazz to blues, folk to rock.

Described as 'Ireland's first female rock singer' in a group known as The Watchtower, she toured Europe and went on to work with many of Ireland's top blues, rock and folk musicians.

Her introduction to jazz came in the early 1980s when songwriter Shay Healy invited her to join with the Jim Doherty Trio in an experimental programme, where musicians from different backgrounds performed together. This was a valuable experience and led to long associations with some of the best jazz musicians around, including Jim Doherty, Noel Kelehan and Louis Stewart.

Her thespian talents have also thrust her into the spotlight, with parts in *Fair City*, *Glenroe*, RTÉ's *Live Mike* with Mike Murphy and Roddy Doyle's gritty *Family*, while she has treaded the boards in the Gasworks Theatre production of *A Streetcar Named Desire* playing Blanche du Bois, the Abbey Theatre's production of *Drama at Inish*, Neil Jordan's *Angel*, The Tivoli Theatre's production of *Blues in the Night* directed by Carol Todd and the part of Grace Farrell in the Olympia Theatre's production of *Annie*, as well as a part in Jimmy Murphy's *Castlecomer Jukebox*, presented by Red Kettle Theatre Company, which toured successfully for five months with an all-star cast.

As a solo performer, Honor has appeared in London's Royal Albert Hall in a celebration of twenty years of The Beatles with the Royal Philharmonic Orchestra and Choral Society, which was attended by Queen Elizabeth and Prince Philip. Additional performances include Shane Connaughton's *Divisions* and Tom Murphy's *Blue Macushla*. She has worked with the BBC Big Band and recorded two concerts for radio with them. She appears regularly at the Cork Jazz Festival and remains one of the most popular attractions there.

Honor has recorded three solo albums *Stormy Waters*, *Chasing the Moon* (with long-time musical collaborator Noel Kelehan, which featured Peter Ainscough, Richie Buckley, Mike Nolan and Martin Curry) and *Fire and Ice*, which was produced by Stephen Keogh, with Barry Green on piano, Jeremy Brown on bass and Stephen Keogh on drums. It has been widely received as her finest album to date.

*Liam Clancy*

# The Dutchman

*Written by Michael Smith*

*Taken from the album* The Makem and Clancy Collection

I first came across the song 'The Dutchman' back in 1972. I was in Chicago and met a guy called Michael Smith who was playing in a public house called The Quiet Knight. It was situated in a bit of a rough and dangerous area, but he braved his way past the Alsatian dogs to find his way through to the dressing room, and it was there that the words of this song came to him.

It's not an Irish song, but it is a lovely song of love. It's about an old couple living in Amsterdam and the husband is a bit confused – maybe he has the onset of Alzheimer's – and he likes to go down to the canal and shout to the fishermen, and he longs to go and take a barge back to Rotterdam. It's really about the love between the man and his wife. She has to come and bring him home, and she puts a drop of whiskey in his tea to calm him down.

The song paints a picture of a day in the life of this old couple, and it's an amazing song because I always sing it live, and even if I've just performed a funny or a lively song, as soon as I start this one, for those three minutes the audience is transfixed. When I look down into the crowd after the song, people are hugging each other and weeping, and that is an amazing feat for any song-maker to accomplish.

'The Dutchman' is the kind of song that if I don't perform it at a show I get into trouble — that and 'The Band Played Waltzing Matilda'!

## The Dutchman

*The Dutchman's not the kind of man*
*To keep his thumb jammed in the dam*
*That holds his dreams in*
*But that's a secret only Margaret knows*

*When Amsterdam is golden in the morning*
*Margaret brings him breakfast*
*She believes him*
*He thinks the tulips bloom beneath the snow*
*He's mad as he can be but Margaret only sees that sometimes*
*Sometimes she sees her unborn children in his eyes*

*Chorus*
*Let us go to the banks of the ocean*
*Where the walls rise above the Zuiderzee*
*Long ago, I used to be a young man*
*And dear Margaret remembers that for me*

*The Dutchman still wears wooden shoes*
*His cap and coat are patched with love*
*That Margaret sewed in*
*Sometimes he thinks he's still in Rotterdam*
*He watches tugboats down canals*
*And calls out to them when he thinks he knows the captain*

*'Til Margaret comes to take him home again*
*Through unforgiving streets*
*That trip him though she holds his arm*
*Sometimes he thinks that he's alone and calls her name*

**Chorus**

*Let us go to the banks of the ocean*
*Where the walls rise above the Zuiderzee*
*Long ago, I used to be a young man*
*And dear Margaret remembers that for me*

*The windmills whirl the winter in*
*She winds his muffler tighter*
*They sit in the kitchen*
*Some tea with whiskey keeps away the dew*
*He sees her for a moment, calls her name*
*She makes the bed up humming some old love song*
*She learned it when the tune was very new*
*He hums a line or two, they hum together in the night*
*The Dutchman falls asleep and Margaret blows the candle out*

**Chorus**

*Let us go to the banks of the ocean*
*Where the walls rise above the Zuiderzee*
*Long ago, I used to be a young man*
*And dear Margaret remembers that for me*

## BIOGRAPHY

The youngest of the Clancy brothers, Liam was born and raised in Carrick-on-Suir, County Tipperary. He was noted as being both creative and musically talented from an early age and spent many hours writing and painting. He was bitten by the acting bug, and, barely out of his teens, he founded the local dramatic society and produced, directed, set-directed and starred in *The Playboy of the Western World*.

In the mid-1950s, American song collector Diane Hamilton arrived at the Clancy home while on a quest for songs. She teamed up with Liam, and the pair travelled to County Armagh, where they encountered singer Sarah Makem and her son, Tommy. This was the beginning of a partnership and a friendship that would last many years. Liam and Tommy both emigrated to America the following year, pursuing careers in acting, both on stage and television.

The Clancy Brothers & Tommy Makem began recording together on Paddy Clancy's Tradition label in the late 1950s, and a record-breaking-sixteen minute long performance on *The Ed Sullivan Show* launched the group into stardom. The four-piece group recorded numerous albums for Columbia Records and enjoyed great success during the 1960s folk revival.

By the early 1970s, Liam gave in to his desire to go solo and left the group. He rapidly established a reputation and, with his own television series, bagged a Canadian Emmy Award.

He later reunited with Tommy Makem, and as Makem & Clancy, the pair recorded several hits including 'The Band Played Waltzing Matilda' and 'The Dutchman'. Together they toured and recorded until the late 1980s, producing numerous albums including *Tommy Makem & Liam Clancy*, *Two for the Early Dew* and *We've Come a Long Way*. His solo offerings include *Irish Troubadour* and *The Dutchman* as well as two volumes of *Liam Clancy in Close Up*.

In later years, Liam rejoined his brothers and nephew Robbie O'Connell, while continuing to perform with his Fairweather Band as well as with the Phil Coulter Orchestra. He welcomed his son Donal into the fold along with Robbie, and together, the group known as Clancy, O'Connell, & Clancy, delighted audiences across North America and Europe, going on to release two highly praised albums.

Liam currently performs as a solo act at pubs, theatres and festivals across North America and Ireland. He is also completing work on his autobiography. He runs his own recording studio at his estate in Ring, County Waterford.

*Marian Bradfield*

## The Emperor's Field

*Written by Marian Bradfield*

*Taken from the album* The Emperor's Field

'The Emperor's Field' is the title track of my third album, and I'd like to pick it for inclusion in this book. It's a song that means a lot to me. It's about a place where I felt loved and safe and secure as a young child, and I have great memories of that time.

I come from Tramore, County Waterford, and there was a huge field beside where my granny lived, and I used to go there to play during the summer holidays. It was a place where you could be anyone you wanted to be – you could hide, you could be free.

The song is not just about my childhood but also, in a way, about the close relationship I had with my granny, who was a lovely, small, warm woman. She had the image of the typical Irish granny. That song brings me back to being hugged by her and settling into that special little space in her neck, where her skin was all soft and warm. It was a safe place and a safe time.

I heard someone on the radio one morning talking about 'the Emperor's field' and I just thought 'that's the title for my song.'

I returned to that field a few years ago to take a photograph, and it was very different and had been built upon, but it's a place that is full of happy memories.

## The Emperor's Field

*Memories are like toys that years ago were made to last*
*Wooden forts and dolls with pretty eyes of coloured glass*
*In long tall grass those bouncing little heads*
*They looked so weird*
*As we chased the breeze with amazing ease*
*Up and down – in the Emperor's field*

*A tree it was your castle*
*Its tallest branch it was your throne*
*And its summer leaves could hide you*
*When you were sad and had to be alone*
*Oh the freedom was so good, the winters long and so unreal*
*And you could hardly wait for the summer days*
*To go back to the Emperor's field*

*Chorus*
*But times do they have to move on*
*And things do they have to change*
*Sometimes it's slow but other times*
*Move so fast you can feel the pain*
*And there's no more sneaking torches*
*Into bed to read late at night*
*No collecting things – no cowboy dreams*
*Its just you and the night*

*When I close my eyes I'm back again*
*And everything's the same*
*I can smell the sea as I watch the lights*
*Sitting up in that old window pane*
*If I had one wish or had a way of making it come real*
*Little Gran I'd sneak back one more time*
*For one last hug in the Emperor's field*

**Chorus**
*But times oh they have to move on*
*And things oh they have to change*
*Sometimes its slow but other times its so fast*
*You can feel the pain*
*And there's no more sneaking torches*
*Into bed to read late at night*
*No collecting things no cowboy dreams*
*It's just me and the night*
*No collecting things no cowboy dreams*
*It's just me and the night.*

# BIOGRAPHY

Marian Bradfield has earned her reputation as one of Ireland's most well-known singer-songwriters and has, together with Loreena McKennitt, Máire Brennan, Hazel O'Connor, Francis Black, Rita Connolly, Mairéad Ní Dhomhnaill and Katy Moffatt, featured on several compilation recordings, including *Celtic Woman 1* and *Celtic Woman 2.*

She has also collaborated with Finbar Furey, Máirtín O'Connor, Jimmy Faulkner, Altan, Liam O'Flynn, Mary Black, Kieran Goss, Aslan, Dónal Lunny, Paddy Glacken, Andy Irvine, Jimmy MacCarthy and The Chieftains, to name a few.

Marian's popularity had led to her being voted by readers of *Hot Press* magazine as one of Ireland's Top 10 female singers and shortlisted by a panel of top music critics as one of Ireland's best solo performers.

She has released three studio albums to date and one live album. Her first solo album, simply entitled *Marian*, was released in 1993 to critical praise from the media. Her second solo offering *Tonight is Just for Us*, was released two years later and resulted in a nomination for one of Ireland's prestigious IRMA Awards.

Two years later came her third solo album *The Emperor's Field*, produced by Pat Donne. This saw her catapulted to fame in the UK and the USA as well as in her native country.

Next came *Marian Bradfield Live*, which was recorded on tour in Holland and launched in May 2004.

*Niamh Kavanagh*

## I Can't Make You Love Me

*Written by Mike Reid and Allen Shamblin*

*Taken from the album* Flying Blind

It's true to say that for pretty much everyone there are songs that become milestones in their life. Be it a romantic song that can later become a first wedding dance, or a song that represents the loss of a loved one. Music is in all our lives, whether we are musicians or not. There are many songs that evoke deep memories for me, happy and sad, but the one that strikes me the deepest is 'I Can't Make You Love Me' written by Mike Reid and Allen Shamblin.

When I was twenty-three, I sat in the National Stadium in Dublin with my best friend Mairead at our first Bonnie Raitt concert. From the beginning, I was swept away, loving Bonnie's sassy attitude, her magnificent playing and her unbelievable voice. During this sensory overload, she introduced a new song and from the opening bars to the very last chord I hardly took a breath. This was the most beautiful song I had ever heard. I felt a sense of loss when it had finished and went straight out the next morning to buy the album. I had to hear it again and again and again.

Allen Shamblin writes that he conceived the song after reading an article about a man who was charged with harassing his ex-wife and was quoted as saying, 'You can't make a woman love you.' When he got together with ex-National Football League player Mike Reid, they created what I think is the perfect song – a song about love, loss and strength. Because only a very strong person can let someone they love go.

When I sing this song, I feel the loss and the depth of love; it reminds me of past loves and disappointments, but strangely enough it reminds me of fantastic moments too. For instance, it reminds me of my great friend Mairead and all that we have shared over the years. It reminds me of when I performed at the Grammies in 1992 with The Commitments and when I watched Bruce Hornsby and Bonnie Raitt perform it live. It brings me back to Nashville when I recorded it for my album *Flying Blind*.

Many people, including George Michael, have recorded it. Even though I sing it myself, there will only be one person who truly owns this song, and that is Bonnie Raitt. I thank her and the writers for giving me so many beautiful memories with each heartbreaking word.

## I Can't Make You Love Me

*Turn down the lights*
*Turn down the bed*
*Turn down these voices*
*Inside my head*

*Lay down with me*
*Tell me no lies*
*Just hold me close*
*Don't patronise, don't patronise me*

*Chorus*
'Cause I can't make you love me if you don't
You can't make your heart feel something it won't
Here in the dark in these final hours
I will lay down my heart, and I'll feel the power
But you won't, no, you won't
Cause I can't make you love me if you don't

I'll close my eyes
Then I won't see
The love you don't feel
When you're holding me

Morning will come
And I'll do what's right
Just give me till then
To give up this fight
And I will give up this fight

*Chorus*
'Cause I can't make you love me if you don't
You can't make your heart feel something it won't
Here in the dark in these final hours
I will lay down my heart and I'll feel the power
But you won't, no, you won't
'Cause I can't make you love me if you don't

# BIOGRAPHY

Niamh Kavanagh has been singing for most of her life, beginning with choirs
and small local bands, training her voice, while at the same time indulging
her love for music.

However, it wasn't until the 1990s that she really came into her own when

*The Commitments* director Alan Parker paid tribute to the north Dubliner's vocal talent by including her on the film's hugely successful soundtrack album.

Niamh went on to sing lead vocals on 'Destination Anywhere', 'Nowhere To Run' and 'Do Right Woman, Do Right Man'. She then toured extensively with the group, appearing at such illustrious events as the 1992 Grammy Awards in New York and the Commitment to Life Concert in Los Angeles.

Then in 1993, before an international audience of over 350 million people, Niamh sang the winning entry for Ireland in the Eurovision Song Contest. The song, 'In Your Eyes', went on to achieve double-platinum status. Having signed to Arista Records, she took her talent around Europe before flying to Nashville, Tennessee, to make her debut album, *Flying Blind*. This album, produced by John Jennings, was released to critical acclaim in 1995 and includes songs from renowned writers such as JD Souther, Bill Whelan and Rodney Crowell. It also features some of the best musical talent that Nashville has to offer, including Mary Chapin Carpenter, who sang backing vocals on several of the tracks.

Since then, Niamh has been touring and performing continually and, in 1997, she recorded her first collaboration album, *Together Alone*, along with Irish singer-songwriter Gerry Carney, which was released in November 1998.

Backed by a single instrument or a nine-piece band in front of fifty or 500,000, Niamh's natural and intimate on-stage presence can be testified by the thousands of music fans who have seen her recent performances in Berlin, Nice, Dublin and Belfast and countless other venues throughout Ireland and Europe.

After a break from music for a couple of years to start a family, Niamh is back on the scene and currently in pre-production for a new solo album.

Jim McCann

*Rebecca Storm*

## Lost Inside Of You

*Written by Leon Russell and Barbra Streisand*

Yet to be released

I'd like to pick 'Lost Inside Of You' from the film *A Star Is Born* – the Streisand/ Kristofferson version.

Back in 1975, I was taken along to see this film. I knew virtually nothing about Ms Streisand as, being only fifteen at the time, I loved all the boy bands instead. I was so impressed by her talent and passion that I went to see the film five times in the same week and bought every recording I could lay my hands on – and learned so much! I also fell madly for Kris and finally met him personally last year at the Olympia Theatre. This duet is so romantic and my partner Kenny and I sing it together in our Streisand Songbook concert. We also played it at our wedding in April this year. As you can see, it not only refers to a love for each other but also the music that connects us and completes the picture. I couldn't imagine sharing my life with anyone who didn't have a passion for music. For me, the words sum up so much how I feel about the relationship we share.

### Lost Inside Of You

*Time has come again*
*And love is in the wind*
*Like some music in dream*
*You made 'em all come true*
*When you came inside my life*
*Now I'm lost inside of you*
*Lost in the music and lost in your eyes*
*I could spend all of my time*
*Hearing songs you sing*
*Feelin' love you bring to me*
*Darlin' bein' close to you*
*Made all my dreams come true*
*When you came inside my life*
*Now I'm lost inside of you.*

## BIOGRAPHY

After studying music and drama, Rebecca Storm formed her own band and toured Europe with a diverse and addictive range of folk and rock songs.

Her obvious love of and passion for musicals then became evident in the impressive list of famous productions she went on to star in, beginning in her early twenties. She auditioned for *Blood Brothers* when she was twenty-three, and, though, she was understandably too fresh-faced to be convincing as Mrs Johnson, author Willy Russell was so taken with her powerful voice that he successfully 'aged' her with the aid of a lot of make-up!

Her performance gained rave reviews, and Rebecca was suddenly, quite dramatically, catapulted into the limelight. This led to a variety of golden opportunities to shine on stage, and there followed prestigious roles in some of the world's most well-known musicals, including Eva Peron in *Evita*, Fantine in *Les Misérables*, Grizabella in *Cats*, Florence in *Chess*, Rose in *Aspects of Love*, Edith Piaf in *Piaf* and Joan of Arc in *Jeanne*.

Her recording career also took off in the mid-1980s, with her single 'Putting On The Show' entering the Top 20. This was closely followed by 'Mr Love', the soundtrack from the David Puttnam film of the same name. Rebecca has received numerous awards for her albums such as *Ovation*, *Broadway by Storm* and *Ireland by Storm*.

She has sung for the King of Norway in Trondheim at his coronation in 1991, while she has also performed several times for the British royal family. In 1992, she devised, directed and starred in *Hollywood Ladies*, a fitting tribute to the many leading ladies who had influenced her career in showbiz – Barbara Streisand, Judy Garland, Julie Andrews and Gracie Fields.

In 2000, she released *I Want To Know What Love Is* (featuring 'I Want To Know What Love Is', 'Gently Breaks My Heart', 'I'm Your Medicine', 'Why Worry', 'I Can Let Go Now', and 'I Still Believe In You'), followed three years later by *Celtic 'n' Broadway*. This saw her collaborate with sixty musicians and was conducted by Harry Rabinowitz who described Rebecca as 'the girl with the voice of a sexy angel'!

Other recordings include 'Don't Cry For Me Argentina', 'High Flying Adored', 'All I Ask of You', 'I Know Him So Well', 'Galway Bay/Sweet Carnlough Bay/Bantry Bay', 'Look What Happened To Mabel', 'Wherever He Ain't', 'Spinning Wheel'.

Rebecca enjoyed great success in 2006 when she took to the stage in Dublin's Gaiety Theatre to bring to life many of Barbra Streisand's greatest hits, including 'Woman In Love', 'Guilty', 'The Way We Were' and 'You Don't Bring Me Flowers Any More'.

*Seán Keane*

## Erin's Lovely Home

*Traditional Song*

*Taken from the album* All Heart No Roses

'Erin's Lovely Home' is a traditional song and was probably the first song that made me aware of my musical surroundings and of growing up in a musical family.

The reason it sticks in my mind is because when I was a child of maybe six or seven, I was playing in my grandmother's thatched house one summer and I was running through the house. There was a man there called Ulick McDonald who lived down the road, and he was in visiting my grandmother. She was someone who used to gather a lot of songs and take down words from people who would visit. Ulick was going blind at the time, and she was writing out the words of this song, and an argument broke out between the two of them as to whether the song was right or the melody was right. The argument was about the last part of the song:

> There are seven links upon my chain
> And every link a year,
> It's then I can return again
> To the arms of my dear.

The two were getting hot and heavy arguing about this part of the song, and this was what really brought it to my attention and made me stop and listen. The result of the argument was that my grandmother took the piece of paper that she was writing the song on and she threw it into the open fire!

That was basically the end of the song until about sixteen years ago I was out in Inishbofin, off the Galway coast. It was in January, when we used to organise a musical weekend every year. I was with a man called Michael Joe Holloran. We had a session one night, and he sang 'Erin's Lovely Home', and that was the first time I had heard it since I was a child. I got the words from him and went to my aunt, and I got the melody that she had for the song and I recorded it on my first album.

I don't know who was right or wrong in the argument, because neither my grandmother nor her neighbour lived to hear me record it. My memory of that day would have been fairly vague, but I'll never forget that line. It was really the first time that I became conscious of the music in my family background.

## Erin's Lovely Home

> When I was young and in my prime,
> The age being twenty-one,
> I acted as a servant to
> A noble gentleman.
> I served him true and honestly,
> And 'tis well it's known,
> But cruelly, he banished me
> From Erin's lovely home

The reason for my banishment,
I mean to let you know,
It's true I loved his daughter
And she loved me also.
She had a very large fortune
But riches I had none,
And that's the reason I must go
From Erin's Lovely Home.

It was in her father's garden,
All in the month of June,
Viewing these fine roses,
All in their youthful bloom.
She said, 'My dearest Willy,
If along with me you'll roam,
We'll bid farewell to all our friends
And Erin's Lovely Home.'

We landed into Belfast town,
By the break of day,
My true love, she got ready
Our passage for to pay.
Five thousand pounds she counted down,
Saying, 'This will be your own,
For we never can return again
To Erin's lovely home.'

But to our sad misfortune,
I mean to let you hear,
It was in the few hours after
Her father did appear.
He brought me back to Omagh Jail,
In the County of Tyrone,
There I was tried and banished

*From Erin's Lovely Home.*
*As I laid under sentence,*
*Before I went away,*
*My true love, she stepped up to me*
*And this to me did say.*
*'Cheer up my dearest Willy,*
*It's you I'll ne'er disown*
*Until you return again*
*To Erin's Lovely Home.'*

*The parting with my own true love*
*Grieves my heart full sore,*
*But the parting with my native home*
*Grieves me ten times more.*
*There are seven links upon my chain*
*And every link a year,*
*It's then I can return again*
*To the arms of my dear.'*

## BIOGRAPHY

Seán is a member of the Keane family from Caherlistrane, County Galway, arguably one of the most famous traditional music families in Ireland.

His own record speaks for itself, however, and it's an impressive and unrivalled one when it comes to the folk, traditional and country music scene. The little boy who witnessed the minor row over the lyrics of 'Erin's Lovely Home' grew into a enthusiastic teenager who collected All-Ireland titles for singing such songs. His early career saw him perform with Shegui, Reel Union and Arcady.

Seán has been on the billing in many prestigious world festivals, including the Cambridge Folk Festival, the Galway Arts Festival, Tonder in Denmark and Lowell in America. In autumn 1999, his performance of The Beatles classic 'Blackbird' at a series of concerts in Dublin's National Concert Hall hosted by the 'fifth Beatle', Sir George Martin, led to Martin offering him the musical arrangement of the song for his fourth album *The Man that I Am*.

In little over a decade, he has produced eight solo albums: *All Heart No Roses, Valley of the Heart, Seansongs, A Portrait: The Best of Seán Keane, The Man that I Am, No Stranger, Turn a Phrase* and *You Got Gold*.

Seán's traditional work has featured in many ways – 'May Morning Dew' was used as part of the soundtrack for the docufilm *The Irish Empire*, while 'Stór Mo Chroí' was included in the soundtracks of two other US documentaries.

*You Got Gold,* his eighth solo album, released in 2006, features eleven new recordings, including the title track 'The Sweeter The Kiss', 'The Penny Falls', 'Shingle by Shingle', 'The Winning Side', 'River Of Yesterday', 'Only Here For A Little While', 'Even Heaven Has To Cry', 'Troublesome Water', 'My Darlin' Hometown' and 'There Are More Questions Than Answers'.

The album has an impressive line-up of gifted musicians, including Arty McGlynn and John McLoughlin on guitars, Rod MacVey on keyboards, Liam Bradley on drums and percussion, Máirtín O'Connor on accordion, Paul Moore and Damian Evans on bass, Rick Epping on harmonica, Seán Regan on fiddle and backing vocals and Deann Whelan on harmonies. The album was produced by Jim Rooney and Seán himself.

## Steve Wall — The Walls

### Something's Wrong

*Written by Steve Wall*

*Taken from the album* Hi-Lo

I wrote this song a few years ago, and it's really a song about the break-up of a relationship. It's about a relationship on the rocks, and it was inspired by a walk I took one day in Salthill, Galway. The sun was shining and I could see the various couples sitting in cars, and it was very easy to see which of the couples were getting on and which were rowing! The ones who were rowing were sitting in stony silence and looking ahead at the ocean or at the horizon.

I decided to write the song using the analogy of a car breaking down and the engine overheating and asking the question, 'Should we jump ship before the engine combusts or take a chance and risk all of the stresses and hurts that come with a relationship?' It's a song that we have always loved performing and it always gets a fantastic reaction from crowds at live gigs.

## Something's Wrong

*Something's wrong*
*We're stranded by the road*
*Can't go on the radiator's blown*
*Silent shapes in the dashboard light*
*Alone in their space, silhouettes in flight.*

*Something's wrong*
*We don't see eye to eye*
*Takes so long to understand just why*
*Evacuate, the engine has caught fire*
*It's not too late to save our precious lives*
*Something's wrong*

*Something's wrong*
*I feel I'm in a cage*
*Can't go on I'm too numb to manage rage*
*I believe the end is always near*
*And I believe the coast is never clear.*

*Someday I may say that I won't be coming home.*
*On a clear day when the weatherman was wrong*

*Something's wrong.*

## BIOGRAPHY

Brothers Steve and Joe Wall had just returned to Ireland from two years spent living in London when they performed their first Walls gig in September 1998, along with new recruits Carl Harms and Rory Doyle.

It was a testing time – the band had recently changed the whole vision of their identity. Previously known as The Stunning, they had taken the brave step of starting from scratch again – with a new band, new name, new members and new music – something they were obviously apprehensive about.

They were one of the first bands in the country to take this risk and set up their own label. On Earshot Records (later changed to Dirtbird Records), they released a string of singles and an EP before their debut album *Hi-Lo* was launched in May 2000. Today, it has reached gold status in Ireland, and many of the songs have featured on countless Irish film and television sound-tracks such as *Dead Bodies*, *Goldfish Memory*, *On the Edge* and the award-winning television series *Bachelor's Walk*.

A chance encounter in the summer of 2001 led to U2 frontman Bono asking the band to support U2 at their second sell-out concert in Slane Castle. Unsurprisingly, they accepted the challenge and played to their biggest crowd ever that day – a mammoth 80,000 people – and were subsequently invited to support the Red Hot Chili Peppers in Lansdowne Road stadium in Dublin.

'To The Bright And Shining Sun' was their next release, which became the most played song on radio by an Irish act during the summer of 2002 and reached No. 11 in the Irish charts.

It was around this time that the group decided to take a leap of faith and build their own studio in Dublin. In order to fund the work, they re-released The Stunning's first album *Paradise in the Picturehouse* on their own label, as it was no longer available to buy. Ironically, The Walls were temporarily put on hold while the lads concentrated on making The Stunning project a success. Although this was a long and drawn-out process, it paid off, and the album charted at No. 2 on the week of release and helped provide the capital to make The Walls' next album.

In February 2004, Carl Harms left to pursue his own musical interests, and a bass player, Jon O'Connell, was recruited while Steve and Joe concentrated on guitars and vocals.

By March of the same year, the band were firmly spreading their wings and embarked on a two-week tour of parts of Poland, Hungary, Slovakia and the Czech Republic. This proved to be a resounding success and gave them the opportunity to play brand-new material every night to audiences who had never seen or heard of them before.

In April 2004, The Walls went to Studio Black Box in France to record their chosen tracks with producer and ex-The Frames member David Odlum. They wanted to make an album that was about capturing the magic of a great live performance – four people in a room doing take after take and trying not to lose the soul of the music in the process. In October 2004, they released one single 'The Drowning Pool' to whet the appetites of their fans.

The band decided to call their album *New Dawn Breaking* after the final and longest track on the record, and 'Passing Through' became the chosen single to precede the album's release. The album entered the Irish charts at No. 5 in the first week of June 2005.

*Dominic Kirwan*

## Through The Eyes Of An Irishman

*Written by Terry Bradford*

*Taken from the album* Golden Dreams

Different artists see different things in different songs, and 'Through The Eyes Of An Irishman' is an amazing song because it was written by an Englishman who was very involved in many of Ireland's biggest musical success stories including Phil Coulter, Finbar Furey and Charlie Landsborough. He wrote this song as a way of trying to see the world through the eyes of an Irishman and to explore the fact that, wherever we are in the world, Irish people think proudly of where they come from.

### Through The Eyes Of An Irishman

*When I was a boy around about three*
*I remember my grandfather whispering to me*

*He said 'learn to appreciate all that you see*
*Because one day it will all mean so much to you'*
*Well without realising the word he did say*
*Sure it started me seeing things in a different way*
*Just like the colour of the sun going down on the bay*
*It was a sight I'd never forget*

**Chorus**

*And we'll all meet tonight every child every woman and man*
*For we know in our hearts that we'll always be part*
*Of our proud and wonderful land*
*Yes we'll all meet tonight and we'll sing as loud as we can*
*Of an island so green it can only be seen*
*Through the eyes of an Irishman*

*Oh the days of my youth were spent searching the land*
*And I couldn't believe all the beauty I'd found*
*Like the flowers and the trees rising out of the ground*
*Full of colour and so full of life*
*Well at twenty-four years that's when I started to roam*
*But it didn't take much to remind me of home*
*And I think of all the places and the people I've known*
*And I may never see again*

**Chorus**

*And we'll all meet tonight every child every woman and man*
*For we know in our hearts that we'll always be part*
*Of our proud and wonderful land*
*Yes we'll all meet tonight and we'll sing as loud as we can*
*Of an island so green it can only be seen*
*Through the eyes of an Irishman*

*Well I left Irish shores when I was thirty years old*
*And I sailed to my future of silver and gold*

*But when the rush was over I was out in the cold*
*It hurt my pocket but never my pride*
*Now there's fire in my heart and my memories still strong*
*Oh how I long for the moment how I yearn for the song*
*And how I'm missing the place that I loved all along*
*That I may never see again*

## BIOGRAPHY

While Dominic enjoys international status today with chart-topping albums and successful concert tours, his Irish roots and early musical influences can still be seen in his live shows.

After several years of performing and developing his own individual style, Dominic was signed to Ritz Records, one of Ireland and the UK's leading independent labels. The first fruits of this relationship was the release of a four-track EP entitled *The Green Hills Are Rolling Still,* followed by his debut Ritz album, *Try a Little Kindness.* Further albums followed, and, firmly established as an artist, headlining his own tours, Dominic not only hosted his own television series but also picked up the prestigious BBC Entertainment Media of the Year Award for Easy Listening/Country Music.

It was his album *On the Way to a Dream,* however, that gave him his first chart-topping success, holding the top spot in the UK country chart. This was followed with the top-selling video *Dominic Kirwan in Concert.* The release of the compilation *The Very Best of Dominic Kirwan* marked the end of the first chapter of his career and also proved to be the perfect introduction to his music for many new fans.

In 1999, Dominic travelled to Nashville, where he collaborated with some of Nashville's best-known musicians, under the production of Ronnie Light. This saw the birth of the *Unconditional Love* album, which, once again, catapulted Dominic to the top of the British country charts. He returned to Nashville on two more occasions to repeat the winning formula and recorded *Stone in Love With You* and *Under Your Spell* whilst he was there.

Other titles released by Dominic include the videos *Live in Galway* and his television concert special *The Entertainer*. His double CD *The Very Best of Dominic Kirwan Vol. 2* was released in 2002, and, in 2003, he released a new album *Echoes of Ireland*, containing many personal favourites and evocative songs from his youth.

He tours continually and performs up to 200 shows a year, including a special weekend each year for his most loyal fans – his friends and neighbours in his home town of Omagh.

The future looks very bright for Dominic and, if hard work is a measure for success, then he will continue to be at the top of his game for many years to come.

*Finbar Furey*

## When You Were Sweet Sixteen

*Written by Jim Thornton*

*Taken from the album* When You Were Sweet Sixteen

The song that stands out for me would have to be, without a doubt, 'When You Were Sweet Sixteen', which was a huge hit for us. It was actually written back in 1847 by a Tipperary man called Jim Thornton. He and his wife were very much in love when they went to live in the USA and while they were in Chicago she died, at a very young age.

He wrote this beautiful and amazing piece of music about her – he had a dream about his dead love and he didn't want to let her go. Jim was a comedian and he used to finish his set every night by singing 'When You Were Sweet Sixteen'.

It's a song that is very special to me. My mother used to sing it, and when my father died in 1979, she asked me if I would record it, and it became a huge hit for us all over the world. I really recorded it in memory of my father.

## When You Were Sweet Sixteen

*When first I saw the love light in your eyes*
*I thought the world held naught but joy for me*
*And even though we've drifted far apart*
*I never dream, but what I dream of thee*

***Chorus***
*I love you as I've never loved before*
*Since first I saw you on the village green*
*Come to me in my dreams of love a stóir*
*I love you as I loved you, when you were sweet*
*When you were sweet sixteen*

*Last night I dreamt I held your hand in mine*
*And once again you were my happy bride*
*I kissed you as I did in auld lang syne*
*As to the church we wandered side by side*

## BIOGRAPHY

Born in inner-city Dublin, Finbar Furey is one of a Travelling family that settled in Claddagh Road, Ballyfermot, in Dublin.

By the early 1960s, music, which had always been part of his life, became a permanent fixture when he performed publicly with his brother Eddie and father Ted, most notably in O'Donoghue's on Merrion Row.

The Furey Brothers, as a group, were formed in 1974 and toured the folk clubs, colleges and universities throughout Britain and Europe, building a large following for their haunting music. They became folk legends across the continent and introduced a whole new generation to the joys of Irish music and unintentionally pioneered a pathway for many new-wave Irish traditional and contemporary bands.

The Fureys soon found themselves headlining concerts on major European tours, particularly in Germany, where they were instrumental in the establishment of Germany's very first Irish Folk Festival Tour. As their reputation grew, they developed a following in Sweden, Denmark, Holland, Belgium, France and Switzerland, Canada, the USA and Australia before their success continued with the arrival of younger brothers Paul and George.

'When You Were Sweet Sixteen' was just one of a string of songs that elevated the affable group to worldwide status, along with 'I Will Love You Every Time When We Are One', 'Leaving Nancy', 'Tara Hill', 'Green Fields Of France', 'Red Rose Café' and 'The Lonesome Boatman'. Subsequent albums include *Sweet Sixteen*, *Golden Days*, *The End of the Day*, *Claddagh Road* and *Winds of Change*.

In 2004, after three decades of life within the confines of a band, Finbar decided to embark on a solo career and savoured the opportunity to explore new pastures as a singer, producer and writer. As a solo performer, Finbar has toured extensively in Ireland, Britain and Australia.

*Joe Dolan*

## Make Me An Island

*Written by A Hammond and M Hazelwood*
*Taken from the album* Joe Dolan: The Collection

I was looking for a change of direction when John Woods of PYE Records introduced me to Joy Nichols. She had this song 'Make Me An Island' and wanted me to record it. At first, it didn't strike me as having hit potential but, during the recording session, it grew on me. When PYE Records released the song, Radio Luxembourg picked it as their 'power play' and, within weeks, it was racing up the UK charts, leading to a *Top of the Pops* appearance.

It made No. 3 in the UK charts and almost immediately became a hit all over Europe, Australia, South Africa and Asia. It was the key to appearances all over Europe, and tours followed in Australia and South Africa.

'Make Me An Island' certainly made my day.

Thirty-odd years later, I am still singing it, and it still makes my day!

# Make Me An Island

*Different eyes, different size, different girls every day.*
*Different names, different games took my breath clean away.*
*But I'm changed, rearranged, I'm enlightened and how*
*you have caught me, you have taught me and I'm different now.*

### *Chorus*
*Take me and break me and close all your windows and doors.*
*Shut me off, cut me off, make me an island, I'm yours.*
*Take me away from the world, take me away from the girls.*
*Take me and break me and make me an island, I'm yours.*

*Running round, shifting ground, that's the life I have seen.*
*But I'm tired, uninspired and I've wiped my slate clean.*
*You are mine, I am yours if the Lord will allow.*
*You have caught me, you have taught me and I'm different now.*

### *Chorus*
*Take me and break me and close all your windows and doors.*
*Shut me off, cut me off, make me an island, I'm yours.*
*Take me away from the world, take me away from the girls.*
*Take me and break me and make me an island, I'm yours.*

### *Chorus*
*Take me and break me and close all your windows and doors.*
*Shut me off, cut me off, make me an island, I'm yours.*
*Take me away from the world, take me away from the girls.*
*Take me and break me and make me an island, I'm yours.*
*Take me and break me and make me an island, I'm yours.*

# BIOGRAPHY

The youngest in a family of eight, Joe Dolan was born in Mullingar, County Westmeath. Both his parents had passed away by the time he was fifteen, and, on his brother's advice, Joe started work as an apprentice newspaper compositor with the *Westmeath Examiner*. Music was, however, even at this early stage, a familiar theme running through the household, and Joe and his brother Ben formed a band and together they played the local dancehall circuit.

After completing his apprenticeship with the newspaper, Joe decided to embark on a full-time career in the music business and formed The Drifters Showband, with Joe as guitarist and lead vocalist. 'The Answer To Everything' was released in 1964 and soared to the No. 4 spot in the Irish charts. He could do no wrong, and hit after hit followed, with 'I Love You More And More Every Day', 'My Own Peculiar Way', 'Aching Breaking Heart', 'Pretty Brown Eyes', 'Love Of The Common People' and 'The Westmeath Bachelor'.

The 1970s brought international recognition – 'Make Me An Island', penned by songwriting duo Hammond and Hazelwood, entered the UK charts at No. 3 and, eventually, got to No. 1 in no less than fourteen countries! 'Teresa', 'You're Such A Good Looking Woman' and 'It Makes No Difference' followed, and all entered the Top 10 in Europe and became No. 1s at home. By now, Joe's entourage was gathering momentum along with his hit records, and he and his eight-piece band toured the UK extensively, along with Europe, Israel, South America and South Africa. In October 1973, Joe collaborated with Italian songwriter-producer Roberto Danova to produce 'Sweet Little Rock 'N' Roller'. Subsequent hits followed, with 'Crazy Woman', 'I Need You', 'Sister Mary', 'Sixteen Brothers', 'My Love' and 'Hush Hush Maria'.

In the early 1980s he released 'More And More', followed by 'It's You, It's You, It's You' and 'Take Me I'm Yours'. In the 1990s, Joe set up his own record label, Gable Records, and built a recording studio in Mullingar, making it easier for him to record new material. In 2003, he released 'Ciara' and the album *Endless Magic*, which reached No. 9 in the charts, making Joe the only Irish singer ever to have had Top 10 hits in the 1960s, 1970s, 1980s and 1990s.

In 1999, Joe released *Joe's 90s*, an album of songs including covers of contemporary artists such as Blur, Oasis and Pulp. The album *21st Century Joe* followed and proved to be equally successful.

# Inspiration

*Brian Kennedy*

## Christopher Street

*Written by Brian Kennedy*

*Taken from the album* Get on with Your Short Life

I wrote this song late one night staring down at the Hudson River from my sixth-floor Manhattan window in the year 2000. I'd moved to New York City to be the lead singer in a new revised version of a wee show called *Riverdance*. Just when I thought my life couldn't get more unpredictable and extraordinary, I was approached by John McColgan and Bill Whelan to perform new songs written especially for me in their global phenomenon. I agreed and was signed up for what became nine months with eight shows a week at the Gershwin Theatre on 8th and 51st Street. I'd managed to sublet an amazing apartment in the West Village via my friend Catherine Owens, and it was a dream come true. You see, I'd always wanted to live in NYC at some stage in my life and didn't want to be like Quentin Crisp and wait until I was in my seventies!

Peforming so many times a week in a musical is like going to the gym for your voice, and I wanted to make sure I didn't overdo it. So, late one night after a typical two-show day, I had the urge to just pick up the guitar and play around with it. My voice was a bit tired so I decided to try and see if I could make the guitar sing instead. I'd become very attached to a tuning I'd learned from Joni Mitchell, 'Open D', which means the strings are tuned to the chord of D and it has a gorgeous wide harmonic drone to it without even holding down any strings.

New York really makes you feel part of the world because every kind of person and every hue of skin coexists on the streets. This song is really like a melodic diary. Each day, I would walk the length of Christopher Street to get the 1 or the 9 train uptown to Broadway and, without fail, I would see someone or something worth remembering. One morning, Tom Cruise was shooting a scene from *Vanilla Sky*; another time I saw some of the cast of *Sex and the City* filming in the nearby gym; Lou Reed floated by, Tony Bennett . . . New York is just like that. I was struck also by the weight of history that was all around me. My own apartment building had a plaque that told me it had been the site where they had first split the atom! All of the soon-to-be world-renowned musicians, artists and poets flocked there thoughout the 1960s and haunted the same streets – Dylan, Joni Mitchell, Neil Young, Aretha Franklin, Miles Davis. So much creative genius drawn to one place.

Sheridan Square also has a plaque to commemorate the gay rights movement after a ground-breaking riot that changed the course of gay history. So many important world-changing things have occured there, way before my feet meandered their daily careful wide-eyed path.

I had the song half-finished when I performed it in its raw state, on one of my precious Monday nights off at Arlene's Grocery in the East Village. It was a great way to see how the song was doing, and the reaction of the small crowd was the encouragement I needed to finish it. Sometimes, a live audience is the best magnifying glass of all. The previously invisible verses kind of wrote themselves when I got back to my apartment. In the third verse, I talk about my oldest friend Martin Morgan back in Dublin. Every night I did *Riverdance* I would be in positon on the stage, just after 8 p.m. and, disregarding the time difference, I would think of Martin who'd become a new father and how he'd be trying to get his little daughter to bed at that same moment I would be behind the curtain making sure my cape was not coming loose and getting ready to sing. I felt so privileged at those moments to be where I was, given where our lives had started, so scarily, not that long ago on the Falls Road in Belfast.

The song is a way to make sense of some of those feelings. I went on to write and record another bunch of songs that would become my New York album called *Get on with Your Short Life* – but that's another story for another day.

## Christopher Street

*Christopher Street was busy tonight*
*As I made my way back home,*
*One of these nights I'll turn on the light*
*Like that taxi by the payphone.*

*Well I've been here a week*
*but it feels like more*
*and God knows how long I'll last.*
*I picked up the mail*
*From the hallway floor*
*And I'm finally making peace with the past.*

*Most of my friends are busy tonight*
*Just getting their kids upstairs.*
*How did our lives change so fast?*
*You just never know what's up the road ahead, do you?*

*Sheridan Square was crazy today*
*When I took the train uptown,*
*It started to snow but I just didn't care*
*cause I never dreamed I'd be Broadway bound.*

*Now Christopher Street has quietened down*
*seems even New York needs to sleep sometimes.*
*One of these nights when I turn out the lights*
*I'll find you waiting to love me.*
*One of these nights when I put out the lights*
*I'll thank the stars up above me,*
*On Christopher Street...*

## BIOGRAPHY

Belfast boy Brian Kennedy was born and raised on the Falls Road, Belfast, one in a family of six children. Drawn towards music from an early age, Brian left for London when he was eighteen and signed his first record deal five years later, with the 1990 release of his debut album *The Great War of Words*.

The early 1990s proved a major turning point in Brian's musical career. He was spotted by none other than Van Morrison and was subsequently invited to join Van's own critically acclaimed Blues and Soul World Tour.

During his six-year association with Van, Brian enjoyed the opportunity to perform with some of the greatest musicians in the industry – Joni Mitchell, Ray Charles, Bob Dylan and many, many more.

In 1996, Brian released his album *A Better Man*, spawning the hits 'A Better Man', 'Life, Love And Happiness' and 'Put The Message In The Box', all of which helped propel the album to No.1 in the charts where it remained for many weeks. It went on to achieve quadruple-platinum sales status in Ireland. The album received an IRMA for Best Irish Male Album, and Brian received a *Hot Press*/2TV Award for Best Irish Male Artist.

Then, 1999 brought the release of another No. 1 album *Now that I Know what I Want* with the single 'These Days' (a duet with Ronan Keating) reaching No. 3 in the national Irish singles chart, achieving platinum status.

In 2000, Brian accepted the role of lead singer in the *Riverdance on Broadway* show, and a CD was released by Decca Broadway, featuring Brian's songs from the show.

His next album *Get on with Your Short Life* was released the following year and *Won't You Take Me Home: The RCA Years* was released in Ireland in 2000 featuring twenty-eight of Brian's most popular and requested songs, traditional and contemporary, plus previously unreleased recordings.

In 2002, Brian signed to Curb Records for a six-album record deal with the awaited release of *Get On With Your Short Life*, and later came his BBC series, *On Song*, from which two albums were released.

Displaying a talent for more than one art, Brian had his first novel published in 2004 by Hodder Headline Ireland entitled *The Arrival of Fergal Flynn*, which went straight into the Irish best-seller charts at No.3. His second novel, *Roman Song*, was published in 2005.

The high esteem in which Brian Kennedy is held was evident when he was asked to sing 'You Raise Me Up' and 'Vincent' at George Best's funeral in December 2005. This performance led to the release of a single 'George Best: A Tribute', produced by Curb Records, featuring Brian and Peter Corry.

Brian hit the headlines again when he was chosen to perform Ireland's entry for the Eurovision Song Contest in Athens, Greece, in May 2006 with his own composition 'Every Song Is A Cry For Love'.

Fresh from his participation in Eurovision, Brian released his much anticipated new album *Homebird*, a double-disc CD, which includes fourteen new studio tracks and a bonus disc of remixes and recordings.

*Paul Brady*

## The World Is What You Make It

*Written by Paul Brady*

*Taken from the album* Spirits Colliding

I wrote 'The World Is What You Make It' in New York in the early 1990s and
what I liked about it lyrically was that it had got me into a way of writing that
I hadn't done before very much, which was kind of lateral thinking instead
of linear thinking. What I was trying to do was write a song, a kind of a get-
up-and-do-it type song. I wanted to find two or three little pictures that
would in some funny way illustrate the point I was trying to make.

I went to a boarding school in my teens and I studied Latin and Roman
History and I was always amazed at the story of Hannibal and how he reput-
edly decided to take Rome by bringing elephants all the way through Spain
and France and up to the Italian Alps. Apparently, these elephants were covered
with gold chain-mail, and it was fantastic, and I just wanted to have some
silly, outrageous images. Each verse had no connection to the others, but they
were linked together by the chorus.

I tend to be fairly straight down the line in my writing – a song usually goes through either an event or an emotion for me and, by the end, it either resolves itself or doesn't, but this was totally different. 'Nobody Knows' was another song like that in that it got me into total lateral thinking, and to be honest, those are the songs that I most enjoy singing because they are the songs that take me by surprise. The others songs, whether they're about me or not, tend to be fairly straightforward.

Musically, 'The World Is What You Make It' also took me into two or three different areas of music that I really like. I've always been fascinated by the way West African music changed when it got to Cuba or to Trinidad and how it was affected by Spanish music in places like Brazil and Paraguay. So in this song, the banjo part could be from Paraguay, and it is just a huge discovery of how all this stuff interlinks, and the excitement for me is that it is interlinking through me and I am having a huge blast doing it.

The audiences like the song because the song is really 'up' musically and it's got a lot of movement to it and you can dance to it and it's slightly bizarre and lyrically it's completely unpredictable. Nobody knows what it's about really. It's light but there's a bit of a sting in it.

I write a lot of dark songs, so any time a light song like 'The World Is What You Make It' comes along I welcome it.

## The World Is What You Make it

*I knew this African called Hannibal*
*(Rock it, roll it, send it down the avenue)*
*Went out to see the Roman Empire fall*
*Uh huh? Uh huh?*
*Two thousand elephants in gold chain-mail*
*(Take it, shake it, make it what you wanna be)*
*Them Roman legionnaires they hit the trail*
*Uh huh?*

**Chorus**
The world is what you make it
The world is what you make it

When Cleopatra ruled in Egypt's land
(Jump down, turn around, look at what the monkey did)
She went to find herself a mighty man
Uh huh? Uh huh?
In come Antonio from Italy
(Haul it, ball it, drag it up the pyramid)
He never knew how hot a girl could be
Uh huh?

**Chorus**
The world is what you make it
The world is what you make it baby
The world is what you make it

Don't start to hit me with your 'no can do'
(Bluesin', losin', workin' up an attitude)
Clean up them windows let the sun shine through
Uh huh? Uh huh?
There ain't no happy time without no pain
(Heartbreak, new date, move on up the alleyway)
Pick up them pieces hit the road again
Uh huh?

**Chorus**
The world is what you make it
The world is what you make it baby
The world is what you make it

# BIOGRAPHY

Paul Brady is widely regarded as one of Ireland's most enduringly popular artists and continues to regale crowds young and old with his collection of classic songs, from 'Beautiful World' to 'Nobody Knows', 'The Island' to 'The Long Goodbye'.

A native of Strabane, Northern Ireland, he was raised on a diet of swing, jazz, rock 'n' roll, 1960s pop and motown, blues, R&B and country and western, all topped up with a little bit of Irish traditional music and song!

Identifying his early musical heroes as Jerry Lee Lewis, Winifred Atwell and 'Fats' Domino, Paul took up the guitar when he was eleven and spent his spare time perfecting his skills. He took summer jobs playing piano and guitar in Bundoran, County Donegal as a teenager, but it wasn't until 1965, in Dublin, that he began to develop a repertoire as a singer and performer, joining a succession of R&B and soul bands including The Inmates, The Kult and Rootzgroop, covering the songs of Ray Charles, James Brown, Junior Walker, Muddy Waters, Howlin' Wolf and Chuck Berry.

He went on to join The Johnstons and recorded seven albums with them. His travels brought him from London to New York City, before he returned home to join Planxty, the group that would also launch the careers of Andy Irvine, Liam O'Flynn, Dónal Lunny and Christy Moore. From 1976 to 1978, he played as a duo with Andy Irvine, a relationship that produced *Andy Irvine and Paul Brady*, an album loved at the time and still sought after today.

The next few years saw him establish his popularity and reputation as one of Ireland's best interpreters of traditional songs. His versions of ballads like 'Arthur McBride' and 'The Lakes Of Pontchartrain' were both compelling and memorable. By the end of the 1970s, however, he was having itchy feet, and, after an acclaimed solo folk album, *Welcome Here Kind Stranger* in 1978 which won the Melody Maker Folk Album of the Year, he decided to move on.

Next came *Hard Station* in the early 1980s, featuring his own compositions. A series of well-received albums followed, including *True for You*, *Back to the Centre*, *Primitive Dance*, *Trick or Treat* and *Spirits Colliding*. Touring extensively both as a solo performer and with his own band, he has forged a reputation as a passionate and exciting performer and attracts a dedicated following worldwide.

After many years of writing on his own, in the late 1990s he began to collaborate with other songwriters and, in two years, he penned almost fifty songs. A union with Rykodisc led to the remastering and re-release of six of his previous albums. A 'Best of' collection called *Nobody Knows: The Best of Paul Brady (1970s–1990s)* followed in 1999 and remained in the Irish album charts for thirty weeks.

In 2000, Paul released his first album of new songs since the 1995 *Spirits Colliding*, with an album entitled *Oh What a World*. This album included collaborations with Carole King, Will Jennings, Ronan Keating, Conner Reeves and Mark Hudson.

In 2001, he formed his own record label, PeeBee Music, and the first release on it was a CD entitled *The Missing Liberty Tapes*, featuring a live recording of a Paul Brady concert in Dublin in 1978, the tapes of which had been lost for twenty-three years. This collection also featured Andy Irvine, Dónal Lunny, Liam O'Flynn, Matt Molloy, Paddy Glackin and Noel Hill.

In 2002, Paul's talent was recognised with a six-programme television series featuring his music. *The Paul Brady Songbook* was well received by audience and critics alike and was followed by a CD of a selection of the recordings and a three-hour DVD of the entire series, both on PeeBee Music.

In 2004, Paul recorded in Nashville, the result of which gave rise to the 2005 album *Say What You Feel*.

Paul Brady continues to push out the boundaries, not only of his own talent but of Irish contemporary music in the new millennium.

## Audrey Healy
## and Charlie McGettigan

### We Will Fly

*Written by Audrey Healy and Charlie McGettigan*

*Taken from the album* Stolen Moments

(Charlie McGettigan)

#### Audrey Healy

When Charlie first expressed an interest in putting my words to music, I began to write with a vengeance. Spurred on by the thought of hearing my song played over the airwaves, I wrote line upon line of verse and sent them to him in the hope that one would turn out to be a gem. At the height of my creative phase, Charlie gave me a good piece of advice, and I think that keeping that advice in mind was instrumental in the composition of this song. The advice? 'Don't try too hard to write a song, just let it happen'. That's the way

'We Will Fly' came about. After many hours poring over the computer key-board, searching for the right words to create the best song, I found that 'We Will Fly' came to me quite by accident and from the heart.

It's a song that is special to me for a number of reasons. Of the songs Charlie and I have written together, it is my favourite. It is also the favourite of many of the people I have played it to, and Charlie reports that his audiences also respond well to it. It seems to have a positive and buoyant message, which is ironic when I think of the circumstances in which I penned the lyrics.

When I was writing the song, there was a lot of sadness in my community. People I knew were sick, there were road accidents – all the things that happen every day but never actually hit home until they affect someone close to you. In a way, they too inspired my writing. I created a voice, a person who wanted to rescue those who hurt and transport them to another time, another place; I wanted to be in that carefree place with them. I envisaged a place that was simple, where there was no tragedy, no tears, no fears, no insecurities, no grief, no heartache. Perhaps this was an unrealistic thought, for these are the emotions that make us human and, ultimately, make us capable of that other great emotion – love. But, just for a while, I longed to escape the realities of life and visit a magical fantasy world where the sun shone all day long and where every moment was precious. I also wanted to acknowledge my friends and loved ones in the song, to teach myself to accept their help and kindness and love in the same way that I wanted to reach out to them. I wanted to allow them to 'be my candle in the night.'

People interpret different things in 'We Will Fly' when they hear it or see Charlie perform it live. What 'We Will Fly' means to me is different to what it means to Charlie and to all other listeners.

One friend of mine loves this song because it reminds her of a mutual friend of ours who died from cancer late last year. We both watched Charlie perform this song for the first time the day before our friend's funeral. My friend says that the image of flying to a carefree place would have comforted our friend, and she only wishes he had been here long enough to hear the song being performed.

I like to think he was.

## Charlie McGettigan

'We Will Fly' is a song that has so many interpretations. I've played it at wedding ceremonies, and people have interpreted it to mean that now that they are married they will experience all the happiness depicted in the words. I've played it at an exhibition of photographs of war-torn Africa, and people have said how relevant it was. It's actually about belief in a higher being who will take care of us if we believe in him or her. At least that's my interpretation.

### We Will Fly

*I will take away your heartache*
*I'll take away your pain*
*When you've taken all that you can take*
*I'll help you smile again*

*Come with me and I will take you*
*Soaring through the sky*
*And together,*
*Together, we will fly*

*Let me take you to a perfect place*
*Where no one ever cries*
*Where all your days are happy days*
*Where all your words are wise*

*Where your questions are all answered*
*And no one ever lies*
*And together,*
*Together, we will fly*

**Chorus**
*We will fly,*
*Where troubles cannot find us*
*We will fly,*
*Across the stormy seas*
*We will fly,*
*Leave all our cares behind us*
*And together,*
*together, we will fly*

*Let me be your candle in the night*
*Let me take your hand*
*And bring you safe*
*To the morning light*

*I will always be your haven*
*I'm always here for you*
*All your sins will be forgiven*
*Be they many, be they few*

*Have faith in me*
*And you will see*
*The truth is in my eyes*
*And together,*
*together we will fly*

**Chorus**
*We will fly,*
*Where troubles cannot find us*
*We will fly,*
*Across the stormy seas*
*We will fly,*
*Leave all our cares behind us*
*And together,*
*together, we will fly*

# BIOGRAPHY

**Audrey Healy** is a freelance journalist and has contributed to the *Sunday Independent*, *Ireland on Sunday*, *Roscommon Champion*, *Longford News*, *Westmeath Topic*, *NewsFour*, *Jemma Publications* and several other publications, including Dublin weeklies and trade magazines. A native of Rooskey, County Roscommon, she has already published three books, *St Thérèse in Ireland*, *Dubliners: What's the Story?* and *Contacted* (with co-author Don Mullan).

She is a regular contributor to local radio and has recently begun song-writing with singer-songwriter Charlie McGettigan.

**Charlie McGettigan** started his musical career in the 1960s, heavily influenced by artists like The Beatles, The Rolling Stones and all the high-profile names of that period. In 1968, Charlie moved to Dublin and honed in on the thriving folk scene there at that time. His influences were people like Paul Brady, Dónal Lunny and Andy Irvine. Having played electric guitar up to then, he purchased his first acoustic guitar and concentrated on developing the finger-picking style which is now his stock-in-trade.

Moving to the rural environment of Drumshanbo, County Leitrim, in 1973, Charlie formed the highly successful Jargon group, which went on to win the prestigious Letterkenny Folk Festival, which in turn, led to a recording contract with Polygram records and the release of Jargon's first single 'Bailieboro And Me'. The band went on to record two more singles before Charlie left to pursue a solo career.

Over the following years he released two solo albums before joining forces with Paul Harrington and Brendan Graham to win the 1994 Eurovision Song Contest with 'Rock 'N' Roll Kids'. He recorded *Rock 'N' Roll Kids: The Album* with Paul Harrington, but the duo went their separate ways shortly after its release in 1994.

Charlie has since pursued a solo career, releasing the albums *In Your Old Room* and *Family Matters*. He tours extensively both in Ireland and abroad and his songs have been recorded by many other artists including Dé Danann, Mary Black and Frances Black, Ray Lynam, Daniel O'Donnell, Hal Ketchum, Maura O'Connell and Eleanor Shanley.

Down the years, Charlie has made many television appearances, both in Ireland and further afield and has presented his own television and radio specials for RTÉ and the BBC. He currently has his own weekly radio programme on Shannonside Radio.

In November 2005, Charlie travelled to Nashville, Tennessee, to work with the legendary producer Bil VornDick and recorded fourteen tracks for a new album *Stolen Moments*, which was released in August 2006. Top acoustic musicians Randy Kohrs (dobro), Aubrie Hainie (fiddle/mandolin), Mark Fain (bass), Pete Huttlinger (guitars), Sam Levine (clarinet), Pat McInerney (drums/percussion), Patti Mitchell (vocals) and Chip Davis (vocals) participated in the recordings over a four-day live session. The album contains new songs by Charlie and some written in collaboration with other writers.

*Mike Hanrahan*

## Garden Of Roses

*Written by Mike Hanrahan*
*Taken from the album* What You Know

As youngsters growing up, we were very aware of certain priests with sexual peculiarities, but our innocence and indoctrinated lives would only allow us quiet giggles, nods and winks and pubescent wonder at their antics.

I then had a somewhat uncomfortable experience with a member of the cloth. I think I tried to shout about it. I remember the sensation of being locked in a chamber, with guilt and shame as my companions. These feelings stayed with me for many years. I know now that my experience was nothing remotely close to the horrific experiences recently accounted by victims of serious sexual and physical abuse at the hands of the clerics, but, for many years, I had my secret. I was in my very early teens and I thought God was on my side.

In recent years, we have heard countless sad stories of the indiscriminate abuse of the innocent children in state care and religious seminaries. One particular case, which was very close to home, upset me so much that I had to write something. 'Garden Of Roses' is, I suppose, my catharsis. It is also my gift to those who were severely abused and damaged. 'Garden Of Roses' is essentially a song of healing. It is also a reminder to people that this must never be allowed to happen again. The song has brought me to so many good places and it has introduced me to some wonderful people. The song was adopted by the Wexford Rape Crisis Centre and is published in one of their books and performed at healing services.

The song has truly found its home … and me? Well, I have firmly shut the door on that chamber.

*A river once frozen, deep in the mind, flows on like a river should in the eyes of a child, in the garden of roses, beautiful roses.*

### Garden Of Roses

*In the garden of roses*
*Where you came by*
*Beautiful roses*
*The eyes of a child*
*In your secret desire*
*You cut it all down*
*Now petals lay scattered*
*on tainted ground*
*In the garden of roses*
*beautiful roses*

*How your temple has fallen*
*The walls cave in*
*We witness the sanctum*
*In their evil sin*
*but a river once frozen*
*Deep in the mind*
*flows on like a river should*

*in the eyes of a child*
*in a garden of roses*
*beautiful roses*

*In the garden of roses*
*where you came by*
*In the garden of roses*
*beautiful roses*
*In the garden of roses*

*A river once frozen*
*Down deep in the mind*
*Flows on like a river should*
*In the eyes of a child*
*In the garden of roses*
*Beautiful roses*
*In the garden of roses*
*Beautiful roses*

## BIOGRAPHY

Mike Hanrahan is a native of Ennis, County Clare, and has enjoyed a colourful and flourishing career in the music industry.

He began his professional calling with Maura O'Connell in the late 1970s, in the duo Tumbleweed. Together they performed a mixture of American country songs from Gram Parsons, Willie Nelson, Emmylou Harris and Richard and Linda Thomson. The two became regulars on the Irish folk circuit and appeared at the first Lisdoonvarna Music Festival.

In 1979, he helped Stockton's Wing on the recording of their second album, *Take a Chance*, the title taken from one of Mike's songs. A year later, he joined the group, and Stockton's Wing toured extensively throughout Europe and the USA. He honed his songwriting skills by penning all six songs on Stockton's Wing's ground-breaking and critically acclaimed 1982 album

*Light in the Western Sky*, which included the hit songs 'Beautiful Affair' and 'Walk Away'.

Stockton's Wing were on the road to success and proceeded to appear at all major European Folk festivals, working with Béla Fleck, The Dubliners, Maura O'Connell and Val Doonican on recordings, live shows and television specials.

The year 1985 saw the release of their best-selling album to date, *Stockton's Wing Live Take One*. This album was recorded at the TV Club in Dublin's Harcourt Street with additional material from the Great Southern in Galway.

*American Special*, *Full Flight* and *Celtic Roots Revival* all followed in the 1980s and, in the summer of 1988, they shared the stage with Michael Jackson for two nights as part of Jacko's world tour!

Continuing their success, Sammy Davis Junior invited the band to perform at his Lansdowne Road shows in Dublin.

Over the years, they have made appearances at numerous music festivals including Calgary, Lisdoonvarna, Cambridge, Milwaukee, Chicago Irish Fest, Chicago Navy Pier Fest, Ballisodare, Chiropody, Neon, Edinburgh, Glasgow, Australia Folk Festival and Brosella Festival Brussels.

The early 1990s saw Mike leave Stockton's Wing to pursue a solo career. He subsequently toured with Finbar Furey throughout the UK before releasing his first solo album *Someone Like You* in 1995. The success of this led to an invitation from Ronnie Drew to perform with him on his one-man show *Ronnie, I Hardly Knew Ya*.

This show proved to be a resounding success, with a seven-week run at the Andrews Lane Theatre in Dublin, followed by appearances throughout Ireland and the UK, including the Edinburgh Fringe Festival 1998, and international dates in Israel, Hungary, the Czech Republic, Denmark, Finland and the USA.

In the late 1990s, Mike produced and arranged Ronnie Drew's *The Humour Is On Me Now*, which included his own composition song 'We Had It All'.

In 2002, he released *What You Know*, produced by Sonny Condell, to critical acclaim, featuring a number of very personal songs, including 'Firefighter', which was written in memory of his late father.

The album also includes 'White Vapour Trail', 'Cradled In Your Arms',

'Falling Down', 'Streets Of The City', 'Today', 'From The Blue', 'Indians and Aliens' and 'No One Living Here', which Mike co-wrote with Brendan Graham.

In 2004, Stockton's Wing came together again for a concert in Dublin's Vicar Street.

Mike continued his collaboration with Ronnie Drew, and together they released a live set called *An Evening With Ronnie Drew and Mike Hanrahan* which brought them to Holland, Belgium, Germany, the UK and two critically acclaimed runs at The Irish Arts Centre, New York. The duo then signed up with Abhann Production Company to perform at the Andrews Lane Theatre, Dublin, for a three-week run in March 2005 to coincide with a DVD release of the theatre show.

The lyrics of 'Garden Of Roses' were included in Jackie Hayden's book *In Their Own Words* and is dedicated to victims of abuse and rape and published on behalf of the Wexford Rape Crisis Centre.

These days, Mike is busy as ever and was elected Chairman of IMRO for an uprecedented third term in December 2004. His commitment to IMRO will see him retain the post until December 2007.

He is currently working with Ronnie Drew as a producer and writing new songs with Leslie Dowdall. He is also Music Director for the successful show *The Legends of Irish Folk* which featured Finbar Furey, Liam Clancy, Paddy Reilly and Ronnie Drew.

'Beautiful Affair', which was written by Mike for Stockton's Wing has been voted into the Top 75 All-Time Great Irish Songs by RTÉ Radio and was voted No. 7 in Today FM's Best Irish Song poll for the past 25 years.

Charlie Landsborough

## What Colour Is The Wind?

*Written by Charlie Landsborough*

*Taken from the album* Charlie Landsborough Classic Doubles

Some years back, I was celebrating my birthday whilst playing support for American singer-songwriter Hugh Moffat, at a gig in Southport, England. During the course of the evening, many of my friends arrived and brought me lovely birthday gifts of books, CDs and things like that. Little did I realise that evening that I was to receive one of my best birthday presents ever.

In the audience that night was a fine singer-songwriter from Blackpool, Pete Naden. He came and sat with me at some point, and as we shared a drink he told me he had a wonderful title for me. He said his friend had overheard a young blind child asking his father, 'What colour is the wind?' Pete said 'I've not managed to do anything with it so I'm giving it to you, see what you can come up with.'

I thought the phrase was beautiful and, a few nights later, began the daunting task of composing a song worthy of that lovely title. I was never really aware of the song's potential until I began to play it at gigs and got this wonderful reaction. I am forever grateful to Pete Naden and especially to the little child for the title that inspired the song which brought me the life of music that I'd always dreamed of.

## What Colour Is The Wind?

*What colour is the wind, Daddy?*
*Is it yellow, red or blue?*
*When he's playing with my hair, Daddy*
*Does he do the same to you?*

*When he's dying does his colour fade?*
*Is a gentler breeze a lighter shade*
*Just like his friend the sea*
*The wind feels blue to me*

*When the blackbird starts to sing, Daddy*
*Do the flowers hear him too?*
*When he's pouring out his heart, Daddy*
*Tell me, what do roses do?*

*Do they cast their scent upon the air?*
*And is fragrance just a rose in prayer*
*Giving thanks to God above*
*For the blackbird's song of love*

### *Chorus*
*Blow, wind, blow*
*Wild and free*
*My Daddy says*
*You're a lot like me*

*I know each colour*
*Its shape and size*
*I've seen them all*
*With my Daddy's eyes*

*I know that grass is green, Daddy*
*I've touched it with my toes*
*And snow is purest white, Daddy*
*I've felt it with my nose*

*But my favourite colour has to be*
*The colour of your love for me*
*And Daddy, I've been told*
*That love is always gold*

**Chorus**
*Blow, wind, blow*
*Wild and free*
*My Daddy says*
*You're a lot like me*
*What colour is the wind?*

## BIOGRAPHY

Born in Liverpool in 1941, Charlie Landsborough is the youngest of eleven children born to Aggie and Charles Alexander. His was a close-knit family and he remembers being always surrounded by music. His mother died when he was only twelve, however, and her passing was to have a great impact on the young boy.

As an adult, Charlie juggled his love of music and songwriting with his day job as a teacher but, by 1984, began to feel disillusioned and feared that his musical ambitions might not materialise. However, 'What Colour Is The Wind' was literally to change the course of his life. It was randomly played by

BBC Radio Foyle presenter Gerry Anderson. This subsequently led to an appearance on *The Late Late Show,* and suddenly Charlie was at No. 1 in the Irish charts. This signified the realisation of a personal dream, and he has since gone from strength to strength and is now one of the all-time biggest-selling artists in Irish music history.

Charlie has released numerous albums, including *Once in a While, Movin' On, Further Down the Road, Reflections, Smile, A Portrait of Charlie Landsborough* and *My Heart Would Know.* He has performed at most major concert halls and theatres, including the London Palladium, Labatts Apollo, Birmingham Symphony Hall, Liverpool Philharmonic Hall, Glasgow Royal Concert Hall, Belfast Opera House, Belfast Waterfront, Dublin's National Concert Hall and the prestigious Albert Dock Festival in Liverpool, where the Liverpool Philharmonic Orchestra accompanied him and his band. He played to a sell-out crowd of over 40,000, arguably the highlight of his career.

*Ronan Hardiman*

## Cry Of The Celts

*Written by Ronan Hardiman*

*Taken from the album* Lord of the Dance

'Cry of the Celts' appears at the end of the opening sequence of *Lord of the Dance*, and it was actually a very agonising piece for me to write.

It was back in 1996 and I had met Michael Flatley for the first time in March of that year. I had worked with him previously on a small project and he had asked me to write something big for him for his forthcoming show. It was an incredibly intensive period for me: I had to write 120 minutes of music, and, obviously, the most important part of the show would be Michael's entry onto the stage. It had to be something spectacular that would silence his critics, as it was his first venture out on his own since his days with *Riverdance*.

I was very aware that it was a very important piece of music, and I would tiptoe up to him regularly with suggestions, but it was never quite what he was looking for. The piece had to be incredibly fiery and dynamic, and, with just ten days to go, I was really beginning to panic when it hadn't come together.

I was getting up at five in the morning to start work and continuing until seven or eight in the evening, and then, one day, this tune eventually began to take shape. After all the hassle and long hours, once I stopped thinking about it too intently my subconscious mind set in, and it was done in half an hour! I went up to Digges Lane where Michael was rehearsing and played it to him. When I'd finished he just walked over to me, shook my hand and said, 'You've got it.' That to me was a very important and very proud moment.

I'll never forget 28 June 2005 in the Point Theatre, Dublin – the opening night of *Lord of the Dance*. We all knew we had created something good, but we never knew how good it really was until the very climax of the piece when it was backed by a big orchestra and there were 5,000 people standing up applauding. I was up in the sound box, watching, and I just began to cry with a mixture of exhaustion and relief. It was, for me, my most defining moment of achievement, to see the piece so widely and ecstatically received by so many people.

The scale of the success of *Lord of the Dance* has exceeded all of our expectations. We could never have predicted the global phenomenon that it has become. It has travelled to the USA, the Middle East and all over Europe and there are still three troupes out there, playing to capacity audiences even now, ten years later.

## BIOGRAPHY

It's a far cry from his job as a teller with the Bank of Ireland, which he courageously left in 1990, fuelled by unfulfilled aspirations of making it as a composer – and it doesn't get much bigger than this.

Ronan Hardiman has rapidly made up for those lost years with a string of impressive credits to his name.

By the time he had met his musical partner Michael Flatley in 1996, he had already accepted and completed major commissions from the BBC and PBS (the Public Broadcasting Service) in America, but it was the phenomenal success of *Lord of the Dance* that catapulted him onto the international stage – and he's been there ever since. An offer from Universal Records saw him release his first solo CD *Solas* in 1998, which achieved gold status in Ireland while it entered the Top 10 in the US Billboard New Age chart.

Recognising a winning formula, Ronan nurtured his rapport with Michael Flatley, and, together in 2000, they developed the hugely successful *Feet of Flames* dance show. This toured the world and culminated in an open-air performance to over 100,000 people in Budapest.

In 2001, Ronan released his second solo album, entitled *Anthem*. Again, this made a significant impact on the US Billboard New Age charts.

The following year, he teamed up with renowned producer Chris Neill, to work on material for New Zealand operatic prodigy Hayley Westenra. Her debut album subsequently sold 1.5 million copies worldwide.

In between live performances, he has also salvaged the time to work on a number of television projects, including the award-winning *Natural History* series, *Waterways* and films such as *My Friend Joe,* in addition to well-known commercials.

In May 2004, Ronan rekindled his relationship with Michael Flatley to work on the sensation that is *Celtic Tiger*. The world premiere of the show took place in Madison Square Gardens in September 2005 and marked the beginning of a sell-out world tour.

## Declan O'Rourke

## No Place To Hide

*Written by Declan O'Rourke*

*Taken from the album* Since Kyabram

A friend of mine and I were touring Germany a few years ago for about a week and a half. We were based with friends in Frankfurt but travelled around the country by car, playing shows with very little publicity, so very few people came, but it was a nice little working holiday at the time.

In one particular venue in East Germany, I met a girl who was working there while we were playing. We had a drink afterwards and she seemed very nice. We got on very well. I noticed she had beautiful brown eyes and she told me that one of her friends said they looked green when she was sad. During another of our conversations, I went to light a smoke from a candle and she stopped me. She said that a sailor would die at sea if I did. I thought it was a wonderful turn of phrase and it stuck in my head. Nothing else happened, but we exchanged details, and my friends and I stayed in a hostel that night and left in the morning.

We both liked each other and felt somehow we'd missed an opportunity and expressed this through a few texts and phone calls. We tried to arrange to meet again on one of my days off. At this stage, I was back in Frankfurt, but she said she had a car and would drive over on her day off. It was 400 miles away! I thought she was nuts, but I was glad she came to see me. She stayed with me in my friend's place.

The room I was staying in was huge, full of lots of musical equipment including an old piano. I was sleeping on a temporary mattress, the foot of which lay under this piano, and I liked how the light hit it during the night. One night while staying there, I dreamt I was on a raft and was sailing across the ocean into a very futuristic looking but strangely medieval city on the coast of Spain. I was left with a nice visual picture from the dream, of being on a raft, floating out to sea.

The girl went home again the next day, but we stayed in touch and have been friends since. When I got home the following week, I had in my notebook a few of the lines I had liked the sound of. All were separate and disconnected, but I tried to put them together to see what sort of story could link them. I watched as it grew and in no time at all I had the story in my head. I just tried to let it lead me to wherever it wanted to go. 'No Place To Hide' was the result.

This song is like a kind of short movie to me. It was a little difficult to write because I had a very detailed, visual account of the story in my head and when you're dealing with a song and words, you don't have much time to express everything, so I had to compress the information; everything I said had to pull its weight in order to get the full story in.

I feel like I achieved what I set out to and said everything I wanted to. However, I think it's probably a very cryptic and ambiguous set of lyrics for the average listener. This was a necessary sacrifice, and the song is very special to me. I like the fact that people have to work with the song and use their imagination to figure out what's going on. It's interactive.

Of course, most people will probably come up with a different idea of what's going on or what the song is about, but that's beautiful in itself. It's like everybody renting out the same movie but all seeing a different one, unique to them. People can take what they want from it. I love the sound of it, too, which is obviously equally as important. This song is a good package both musically and lyrically for me.

It begins with the sound of rain. A man is standing on his porch in a wooded area. Nervous. Excited. Waiting for someone. A woman he has never met. His wife to be. He knows she will arrive at any moment, probably in a taxi. She has come a long way from a foreign country; she is most likely an Asian woman, mid to late twenties. She has come for a better life with this man who is considerably wealthy compared to what she is used to, but of average means in his own country. He is German, approaching middle age. A reserved man, well-read, sturdy.

She arrives. They greet each other rather awkwardly and he takes her bags. They are alone. She follows him inside. He leads her into the bedroom and puts down her bags. The room has a double bed and is a normal looking bedroom for a couple. Everything is elegant and white. It hits her that this is permanent and it's as if she's living there already. There are possibly separate wardrobes and lockers, he maybe has some clothes and women's things prepared for her. It feels almost perverse and embarrassing. This is where they will sleep together.

He begins showing her around the house. They go into the living room. It is spacious and quiet. On a table are some flowers. Things are still awkward but both are genuine and hopeful. He lights a cigarette and asks her with gestures, albeit too late, if she minds. She doesn't like smoke but pretends she doesn't mind and turns away shyly, trying to hide her thoughts. Clumsily, he doesn't see it. He stares at her, quite impressed by her beauty and how she holds herself.

Everything is foreign to her. Strange. She has resigned herself to her new life but already she has thoughts of home and loved ones. She is gentle, quiet and a little sad in her new home.

That night they lay down together. The man is asleep fairly soon and content with the new change in his life, everything feels right and he is happy. He dreams of walking along the seashore. He finds a raft and drifts away peacefully on the waves. She lies awake in darkness, the only light coming from the moon, slipping through a gap in the curtains and lighting the corners of an old black piano at the end of the room.

## No Place To Hide

He stepped outside his door
and listened to the air;
The rain was falling all around,
and he knew that she
was near.
She'd travelled many miles to see him,
with everything to gain.
And he had nothing left to lose,
just his loneliness and pain.

He took her bags into the bedroom
where all was cut and dried.
Her eyes were green when she was sad
and felt a little blue inside.
He lit a smoke up on a candle
and somewhere a sailor died.
She said she didn't mind the smell,
and looked away,
as he blew the smoke aside.
But wo, she was pretty when she had no place to,
wo, she was pretty when she had no place to,
wo, she was pretty when she had no place to hide.

She thought about her family and friends
and hoped that she would see them soon again.

She lay awake now in the darkness,
where an old piano glistened in the night.
He dreamt he found a little boat
and sailed away upon the tide.

# BIOGRAPHY

Declan O'Rourke acquired his first guitar at the age of thirteen – a gift from a priest in Kyabram who recognised his love of music and obvious talent. These early days are acknowledged in the title of his debut album *Since Kyabram*, which was released to critical acclaim in October 2004, entering the Irish album charts at No. 5 and being the only new Irish entry in the Top 75 album chart that week. *Since Kyabram* subsequently went gold and then platinum.

Since its release, Declan has completed two sell-out nationwide Irish tours, with the second one culminating in a much-lauded, full-capacity show in Dublin's Olympia Theatre in March 2005.

Declan's songwriting explores many diverse subjects; along with unconventional love songs such as 'Everything Is Different' and 'Sarah', his songs and lyrics cover many generic themes. His songs vary from the slower 'No Place To Hide' and 'Galileo' to the more up-tempo tracks like 'No Brakes' and 'One-Way Minds'.

*Since Kyabram*'s final track, 'Marrying The Sea', ends with an instrumental piece entitled "Til Death Do Us Part', which putting into practice Declan's talent for composing and arranging music.

Declan has performed on the No. 1 selling compilations *Even Better than the Real Thing Vol. 2* and *Even Better than the Real Thing Vol. 3*, proceeds of which went to The National Children's Hospital and Tsunami Relief respectively.

Other career highlights include performing at the first Irish Woodstock in Inistioge, County Kilkenny, playing guitar with Bic Runga on her European tour and opening multiple shows for Planxty during shows at Vicar Street.

*Colm Ó Snodaigh — Kíla*

## Cé Tú Féin?

*Written by Colm Ó Snodaigh*

*Taken from the album* Lemonade & Buns

Ennis worked as an electrician before the war. He, his wife and their children lived a normal, urban city life in Bosnia – they were neither rich nor poor. At night, he sometimes sang in bars – happy songs mostly. But then the war broke out and almost all able-bodied men were drafted into an emergency army to defend the city of Sarajevo.

The electrician became a soldier.

His take-home pay from his new, dangerous, frontline, night-shift job became packets of cigarettes. He sold everything in the house to feed his family. He then got injured when a bullet caught him in the thigh. Miraculously (at the time, he thought), he and his family were airlifted from the war zone and flown to a country that he had only heard of occasionally: Ireland.

The soldier became a refugee.

I met him when both of us were invited by artist Tom Ryan to participate in an art installation by the banks of the Shannon in Limerick City. Myself and Ennis were to sing snippets of songs from either side of a footbridge while a row-boat full of candles was guided under it. The bridge was draped with a netting of a thousand white luminous paper stars.

The finale of the installation saw both of us sing a Bosnian song in harmony together. This was to symbolise the coming together of cultures, the welcoming of strangers to a new land.

When Tom first mentioned the event to me a couple of lines came to me. 'Cé tú féin, a strainséar chaoin?' Who are you, kind stranger?

My journey down to Limerick on the day of the event was an exercise in frantic composition. I spent the whole time writing and rewriting in my head, trying to get the words to sit with the melodies as I kept an eye on the road and talked to Ennis, whom I had picked up in his west Dublin home.

The above three lines remained with me long after the show and when Dee (our fiddle player) said that she was looking for a Christmas song I sang her the lines. And as I sang it, more and more lines came to me. Dee responded to my singing with some beautiful fiddle playing and when it came to recording our album *Lemonade & Buns*, the song flowed effortlessly.

On our journey home I got to know Ennis a little better. He missed his country. He missed the way his life had been. He knew however, that his country had changed forever and he was afraid that it wasn't for the better. He also found it hard being on the dole - he couldn't get a job that would pay as much as he was getting from social welfare. His wife resisted learning English and spent her time watching Yugoslavian TV and his sons had developed Dublin accents and were enjoying Gaelic Football in school.

The refugee, unhappily, was becoming an emigrant.

## Cé Tú féin?

*Cé tú féin?*
*A strainséar chaoin*
*Cé tú féin?*
*An lách no dian*

Do bhuille thréan?
Cé tú féin?
Ar tháinig tú ó
I bhfad gcéin
Aniar aduaidh
Anoir aneas
Ar tháinig tú ó fuacht nó teas?
Cé tú féin?

Tar isteach
A strainséar righin
Tar isteach
Suí chun boird
Ól braon di
Nó lig do scíth
'S inis dúinn
An fáth go bhfuil
Do aghaidh chiúin
Uaigneach dorcha
An fáth go bhfuil
Do shúile
Lán le cuamha

Cé tú féin?
'S im' chuisle
I gcuideachta
Órga 's draíochta
Im' lorg
I leabaidh
I leabhar mór gach míosa
Ní thagaim
Níor tháinig mé riamh
Ar an ní a bhí uaim

'S i ngleannta
I gcoillte
Le scaipeadh na síolta
Mé thuas seal
'S thíos seal
Le suaitheadh gach oíche
Ní bhraithim
Níor bhraith mé riamh
An ní a bhí uaim
'Slán agat
A strainséar chaoin ro

Slán agat
'S guíom gach rath
'S sonas ort
Amach anseo
'S beidh fáilte romhat riamh im chroí
Cé uaigneach
Cé sonasach
Cé meangadh mór na gréine
Ar do aghaidh


## Who Are You?

Who are you
Kind stranger
Who are you?
Are you gentle or aggressive since your traumatic ordeal?
Who are you?
And did you come from far away
From west from north
From east from south

*Did you come from cold or from heat?*
*Who are you?*

*Come in*
*Tense stranger*
*Come in*
*Sit by the table*
*Have a drink or have a rest*
*And tell us the reason why*
*Your quiet face is dark and lonely*
*Why your eyes are full of sadness*
*And who are*

*In my pulse*
*In magical, golden company*
*In my footstep, in beds*
*In the great book of every months*
*I don't arrive or ever come upon*
*What is essential for my needs*

*And in valleys, in forests*
*With the scattering of seeds*
*I fill with hope and then empty*
*With each night's storm*
*I don't feel and I have never felt*

*And goodbye*
*Gentle stranger*
*Goodbye for now*
*And I wish you every success*
*And happiness from here on in*
*And you will always*
*Be welcome inside this heart*
*Whether lonely, whether happy*

*Whether the sun's wide*
*Smile is on your face*

# BIOGRAPHY

A group of enthusiastic and passionate sixteen-year-old music lovers came together in Coláiste Eoin, Dublin, in 1987 – and Kíla was born. In its infancy, the band consisted of Eoin Dillon on the uilleann pipes, Colm Mac Con Iomaire on the fiddle, Rossa Ó Snodaigh on the whistle, Rónán Ó Snodaigh on the bodhrán, Karl Odlum on the bass and Dave Odlum on guitar.

They played their first official gig upstairs in The Baggot Inn in 1987 – to an audience of three! After qualifiying as a physiotherapist, Colm Ó Snodaigh joined for Kíla's first festival in Germany in 1988 while Rónán and Dave finished school.

By 1989, Rónán and Dave had left school and the band juggled gigging regularly in The Baggot Inn with busking on the streets of Dublin, and in 1990, the album *Éist* was released. Recorded by Kíla, it featured eleven songs penned by Colm. This was followed a year later by the album *Groovin'*. Changes were afoot, however, and Dave Odlum and Colm Mac Con Iomaire left to join The Frames. Enter Dee Armstrong on fiddle, with Dave Reidy and Eoin O'Brien on electric guitars. The band were soon making waves in the music scene and performed at the Letterkenny International Festival and Clifton Blues Festival, and in 1993 they released another album, *Handel's Fantasy*. Jazz bassist, Ed Kelly joined after Karl Odlum left, and Kíla completed their first tour of Germany and performed at the Lorient Interceltique Festival in France.

A year later, in 1995, *Mind the Gap* was released, and Colm takes on the role of manager for the band. A new album *Tóg É Go Bog É* was released in 1997, featuring the single 'Ón Taobh Tuathail Amach', which reached No. 24 in the Irish single charts. *Tóg É Go Bog É* was then released in Japan in 1998 through Video Arts and MSI, and in Australia in 1999 with Green Linnet.

*Tóg É Go Bog É* was followed in 2000 with the release of a new album *Lemonade & Buns*. The band also re-released *Handel's Fantasy* and a limited edition *Live* album, recorded at Dublin's Vicar Street. Kíla then went on to win a Meteor Award for Best Traditional Music Act in 2002.

In 2003, they began recording the album *Luna Park,* which was then released and rose to No. 15 in the Irish charts. It was later released with US company WorldVillage and with Resistencia in Spain.

Kíla's profile continued to rise, and in 2004, they performed in fourteen countries, including Sweden, Canada, Japan, Israel, Austria, Denmark, Scotland, New Zealand, Australia, France and Germany. Plankton of Japan released *Luna Park* and *Tonnta Ró,* and while on tour there they played to 40 million viewers on Japan's *News 23* programme. They have performed at many festivals including four Womad festivals, Forum Barcelona and Sziget Festival in Budapest. Kila's *Live In Dublin* album was released in late 2004.

Their albums include *Handel's Fantasy, Mind the Gap, Tóg É Go Bog É, Lemonade & Buns, Monkey* and *Luna Park,* with *Luna Park, Handel's Fantasy* and *Mind the Gap* achieving gold status and *Tóg É Go Bog É* achieving platinum status in 2004.

Colm has written a book of short stories, recorded a solo album and is also working on a second album. He has written for film, theatre and dance companies.

Kíla's latest album *Kíla and Oki*, released in 2006, is a collaboration with Japanese ainu musician Oki and is a blend of traditional Irish and Japanese ainu music.

*Don Baker*

## Chains

*Written by Don Baker*

*Taken from the album* Miss You

I chose this song because it's about codependency and drug addiction. I think this is something that's never really spoken about in society or in the media. People talk about insecurities from their childhood and jealous wives, but they never talk about the root cause of their problems or about the social implications of addiction. This song talks about it.

I'm starting to learn the piano now, and I find it's therapeutic. Music for me is like meditation. Today's music is all about image and hype, and I don't really like that, but when I play, I find I don't think about anything else but the music.

## Chains

I don't want nobody putting chains on me
I don't want love if I can't be free
Don't want to be dependent on no one else
I can have love if I got myself
This addiction is crazy
It's so hard to see
I'll fix you if you fix me
I don't want chains on me
Love chains on me
No more

*Chorus*
I don't want a hostage
Don't want to be a prisoner
I'm not a victim and I don't want chains on me

Cinderella was a junky and full of pain
Ain't that the truth I guess we're all the same
I don't want nobody slowing me down
Nobody's fool no one's clown
This addiction is crazy
It's so hard to see
I'll fix you if you fix me
I don't want chains on me
Love chains on me
No more

*Chorus*
I don't want a hostage
Don't want to be a prisoner
I'm not a victim and I don't want chains on me
No I don't want chains on me

*Chains on me*
*Chains on me*
*Chains on me*

# BIOGRAPHY

Don Baker was born in Whitehall, Dublin. He was hospitalised at an early age and while in hospital discovered the harmonica. Soon after he took up the guitar and, according to himself, 'never looked back.'

Leaving Ireland for Europe, aged twenty-two, Don travelled throughout Germany, Austria, Holland and France, playing all the while. He moved on to jazz and blues clubs and, with the help of a newly acquired agent, got the odd support slot at major concerts. He spent ten years on the road.

In 1979, he was asked by The *Late Late Show* to write a song about inner-city Dublin. He penned 'Dublin's Inner City', which became a huge hit for The Jolly Beggarmen, reaching No. 2 in the Irish charts. Don has since built a wide reputation as a harmonica player in his own right. Mark Feltham is on record as calling him 'the greatest acoustic harmonica player in the world', and he can count Charlie McCoy and U2's Bono amongst his fans.

He is the author of several instruction books on the harmonica as well as five teaching videos. He also adjudicates biannually at the World Harmonica Championships in the blues category. His harmonica-playing is influenced by blues players such as Sonny Boy Williamson and Sonny Terry. He was also greatly influenced by Charlie McCoy, who has since become a friend and recorded the Don Baker composition 'Jordanna'. Don recorded the Charlie McCoy composition 'Funky Duck' on his album, *Miss You*, which also includes 'Chains'. Don learned blues guitar by listening to the great country blues players: Mississippi John Hurt, Blind Blake, Robert Johnson, and Scrapper Blackwell.

Don has many strings to his bow and is also a talented actor. He made his debut in the film *In the Name of the Father* (1994), directed by Jim Sheridan. Don has since featured in many successful films, including *Mia* starring alongside Claudia Cardinale, and *On the Nose,* starring alongside Dan Ackroyd and Robbie Coltrane.

Don has been on the road and has travelled worldwide entertaining audiences for the past three decades. His albums include *No Regrets, No Nonsense, Born with the Blues, Just Don Baker, Miss You, Almost Illegal, Duckin' and Divin'* and the single 'Sea Of Heartbreak', which was written in aid of the Tsunami Appeal after the Asian disaster in Christmas 2004.

*Eleanor McEvoy*

## The Rain Falls Down

*Written by Eleanor McEvoy*
*Taken from the album* Yola

I wrote 'The Rain Falls Down' in January 2003. On this one particular day, everything had been going wrong. I couldn't get out of bed because I had been up so late the previous night the heating wasn't working so it was freezing; there was no coffee, and I couldn't get online to get my e-mails – and I thought I'd feel better if I had someone to take my bad mood out on.

I decided to take it out on the character in the song that I was writing. I thought that if I made the character even more miserable than I was, it would make me feel a lot better, so I thought about everything that had happened to me and put it into the song and then I tried to think of something even nastier that I could do to her.

I started to make up stuff about her boyfriend dumping her – now, if you're familiar with my songs, you'll know that the people in my songs get dumped a lot, but this time I wanted to go one step further, so I thought about figuring out a new way of getting dumped. I decided that she was going to get dumped by e-mail and that made me really happy!

I felt a lot better after I put my misery back on her. I was kind of adopting the Hollywood scriptwriting attitude of 'When your character is in trouble, give them some more trouble'.

Sometimes, you get flashes of inspiration and that gives you the start but then you have to work on the song. I remember getting really excited about this song and running around wildly looking for people to play it too.

### The Rain Falls Down

**Chorus**
*The rain falls, the rain falls down*
*The rain falls, the rain falls down*
*The rain falls, the rain falls down*
*The rain falls, the rain falls down on me*

*Well I gotta get up*
*but I can't get my head out of bed 'cause I went to bed late*
*So I drag myself out*
*and I wonder about how I let myself get in this state*
*And my coffee's run out*
*and the milk has gone off and the last piece of bread has gone stale*
*And I hear myself curse*
*when the heating won't work 'cause I didn't pay the bill right away*

*The cold air is chilling me*
*and my head is killing me and I've only got myself to blame*
*I swear that in future I'll be more together*
*I see my computer, so I go to check my mail*
*It takes me a while,*
*but eventually I get online, and when I finally do*
*I open up my messages*
*the second one's from you... then—*

**Chorus**

*The rain falls, the rain falls down*
*The rain falls, the rain falls down*
*The rain falls, the rain falls down*
*The rain falls, the rain falls down on me*

*So you're breaking it off*
*and you didn't think it could be said to me straight to my face*
*And those rumours were true*
*you've got somebody new, you've been taking her out in my place*
*And now you want rid of me*
*you've gotta be kidding me, don't you think I want rid of you?*
*And no you cannot be my friend*
*My friends they come through... when—*

**Chorus**

*The rain falls, the rain falls down*
*The rain falls, the rain falls down*
*The rain falls, the rain falls down*
*The rain falls, the rain falls down on me*

*Well I click on your mail*
*and I drag it away to the trash and I gather my strength*
*I delete your address*
*all along with the rest of the messages you ever sent*
*'Cause I will find someone new*
*someone who'll love me too, cherish me to have and to hold*
*And you will be the one we'll see*
*Out there in the cold... when—*

**Chorus**

*The rain falls, the rain falls down*
*The rain falls, the rain falls down*
*The rain falls, the rain falls down*
*The rain falls, the rain falls down on me*

# BIOGRAPHY

There were no prizes for predicting the career path of the angelic four-year-old who confidently mounted the stage to perform at an Irish music competition as the lead singer in her sister's band. By the age of eight, Eleanor was playing the violin and was a pupil of the College of Music in Dublin for both piano and violin until 1985.

The next stage in her musical training brought her to Trinity College in Dublin where she studied music by day and worked in pit orchestras by night. She graduated with an honours degree and was accepted to the National Symphony Orchestra of Ireland, with whom she worked for five years before making the brave decision to leave the classical world behind her and indulge her passion for songwriting.

The release of her own composition 'Only A Woman's Heart' in 1992 saw her elevated to star status in Ireland, and it became the inspiration song for the *A Woman's Heart* anthology album, which has since become one of the best-selling albums in Irish history and stayed in the Top 10 for over a year.

Then 1994 saw the worldwide release of her self-titled debut album *Eleanor McEvoy* on Geffen Records. She subsequently brought her soothing voice and unique style of songwriting to the USA, Europe and the Far East to support the album, building up a loyal fan base and racking up international sales.

In 1996, she released *What's Following Me?* This release featured the single 'Precious Little'. She toured extensively again, playing to sell-out venues in the USA and Europe. Her second single, 'Whisper A Prayer To The Moon' was included on the soundtrack of the Pierce Brosnan movie *The Nephew*, which was released in 1998. She later performed 'The Seabird' for the soundtrack of *Some Mother's Son* staring Helen Mirren, which was written by *Riverdance* composer Bill Whelan.

Eleanor released her third album *Snapshots* in 1999. Produced by Rupert Hine, it received rave reviews on both sides of the Atlantic. This album and a subsequent international tour for its promotion led to her collaboration with Belfast pianist Brian Connor.

As a songwriter, Eleanor has had her songs covered by artists as diverse as Emmylou Harris, Phil Coulter and Mary Black.

Her albums include *Early Years*, *Eleanor McEvoy (Special Edition)*, *Portrait of a Songwriter*, *Yola*, *Snapshots* and *What's Following Me?*

*Brendan Bowyer*

## The Holy City (Jerusalem)

*Music by Stephen Adams / Words by Frederick E Weatherly*

*Taken from the album* On Higher Ground

A song that has played an important part in my career is 'The Holy City', popularly called 'Jerusalem'. I've recorded it three times, most recently on an album with Universal called *On Higher Ground*.

To explain why concert songs like 'The Holy City' were included in the repertoire of the Royal Showband is probably to explain something of the golden era of showbands, which I believe was between the time when Elvis was inducted into the army in 1958 and the arrival of The Beatles in the summer of 1962. Showbands were on fire! – and were expected to provide dancing, showtime and, most importantly – boy meets girl!

In Christmas 1960, we introduced 'The Holy City' as a concert number as part of showtime, and it received huge acclaim. I've been singing it ever since.

'The Holy City' means more to me than just a standard tenor solo. I eventually came to treat it dramatically; I became submerged in the music and lyrics and acted it out as I sang and felt it. This probably could be said of many other tenor solos I've touched on through the years, but 'The Holy City' was the greatest vehicle of them all.

## The Holy City (Jerusalem)

*Last night I lay a-sleeping,*
*There came a dream so fair,*
*I stood in old Jerusalem,*
*Beside the temple there.*
*I heard the children singing,*
*And ever as they sang,*
*Methought the voice of angels*
*From Heav'n in answer rang.*
*Methought the voice of angels*
*From Heav'n in answer rang.*

*Chorus*
*Jerusalem, Jerusalem,*
*Lift up your gates and sing;*
*Hosanna in the highest,*
*Hosanna to your King.*

*And then methought my dream was changed,*
*The streets no longer rang.*
*But with a glad Hosanna*
*The little children sang.*
*The sun grew dark with mystery,*
*The morn was cold and chill,*
*But the shadow of a cross arose*
*Upon a lonely hill.*
*But the shadow of a cross arose*
*Upon a lonely hill.*

*Chorus*
*Jerusalem, Jerusalem,*
*Hark, how the angels sing*
*Hosanna through the ages,*
*Hosanna to your King.*

*Then once again the scene was changed,*
*New earth there seemed to be.*
*I saw the Holy City*
*Beside the timeless sea.*
*The light of God was on its streets,*
*The gates were open wide;*
*And all who would might enter*
*And no one was denied.*
*No need of moon nor stars by night*
*Or sun to shine by day,*
*It was the new Jerusalem*
*That would not pass away.*
*It was the new Jerusalem*
*That would not pass away*

*Chorus*
*Jerusalem, Jerusalem,*
*Sing for the night is o'er;*
*Hosanna in the highest,*
*Hosanna for ever more.*
*Hosanna in the highest,*
*Hosanna for ever more.*

# BIOGRAPHY

Born in County Waterford, Brendan Bowyer is synonymous with the magic of the showband era and first came into prominence in 1959 as lead singer with the famous Royal Showband from the city of his birth.

His recordings with the Royal include six No. 1 hits, the most successful being 'The Hucklebuck', which went platinum internationally. The 1960s were the golden era when the Royal Showband staked their claim as Ireland's most popular showband. In 1961, they were voted the No. 1 Modern Dance Band in the UK and made the movie *The One Nighters*, which received a Special Award at the Cork Film Festival in 1963.

The 1980s saw Brendan juggle performing in Las Vegas with sell-out summer seasons at Clontarf Castle in Dublin. One of the most treasured memories of the 1970s was undoubtedly when the King himself, Elvis Presley, came to see them perform. Elvis was so impressed with Brendan's performance of 'You Gave Me A Mountain', that he later recorded it himself and included it in his own programme and also featured it on his worldwide special: *Aloha From Hawaii*.

Brendan made a welcome return to the recording studio in the 1990s and recorded the appropriately titled *Best of Brendan Bowyer*, which included all his hits, including 'The Hucklebuck'. The next release was *Going Home*, a diverse collection of old and new songs, which accentuated his versatile skills, followed by *Brendan Bowyer's Ireland*, a compilation of his favourite Irish ballads.

His long-awaited revival came in 2001 with the release of *The New Century* and the subsequent release of the album *Follow On*, his own tribute to some of Ireland's best-known singer-songwriters.

He continues to tour and perform with an enviable zest for life and is now joined by his daughter Aisling.

*Mary Coughlan*

## The Magdalen Laundry

*Written by Johnny Mulhern*

*Taken from the album* Sentimental Killer

*Recorded by Mary Coughlan and Eleanor Shanley*

I first told Johnny Mulhern about the Magdalen Laundry in Galway. When I was a teenager, a favourite pastime was to walk up the town every evening after school, with the school uniform skirt hitched up as high as was decent. On one or two evenings, we would pass by the Magdalen Laundry and see girls walking with nuns. They always looked really sad and were always looking at the ground. Nobody in the adult world would ever give us a straight answer as to who they were or why they were there with the nuns.

Over time, I came to know who they were and why they were there: they were unmarried pregnant girls who worked in the laundry. There were lots of stories about the place, and a girl, whose family owned a pub that backed onto a laneway beside the laundry, had heartbreaking stories about girls running away, being found and brought back.

Johnny Mulhern's song is, in my opinion, the greatest piece ever written about the subject. I still get very emotional and angry when I'm singing it. People cry a lot when they hear it. In fact, I know someone who teaches English to foreign students. In school, she plays the song and will then ask the students if they know what it is about.

She does this every year and when she tells them, every year, about 80 per cent of the class just cry.

## The Magdalen Laundry

*For seventeen years I've been scrubbing this washboard*
*Ever since the fellas started in after me*
*My mother poor soul didn't know what to do*
*The Canon said 'Child, there's a place for you'*
*Now I'm serving my time at the Magdalen Laundry*
*I'm towing the line at the Magdalen Laundry*

*There's girls from the country, girls from the town*
*Their bony white elbows going up and down*
*The Reverend Mother as she glides through the place*
*A tight little smile on the side of her face*
*She's running the show at the Magdalen Laundry*
*She's got nowhere to go but the Magdalen Laundry*

*Chorus*
*Oh Lord won't you let me? don't you let me?*
*Won't you let me wash away the stain?*
*Oh Lord won't you let me wash away the stain?*

*I'm washing altar linen and cassocks and stoles*
*I'm scrubbing long johns for these Holy Joes*
*We know where they've been when they're not saving souls*
*What the red wine split, what the smooth hand poured*

*We're squeezing it out at the Magdalen Laundry*
*We're scrubbing it out at the Magdalen Laundry*

**Chorus**
*Oh Lord won't you let me, don't you let me*
*Won't you let me wash away the stain*
*Oh Lord won't you let me wash away the stain*

*Sunday afternoon when the Lord's at rest*
*It's off to the prom to watch the waves roll by*
*We're chewing on our toffees, hear the seagulls squawk*
*'There go the Maggies,' the children talk*
*Through our faces they stare at the Magdalen Laundry*
*In our eyes see the glare of the Magdalen Laundry*

**Chorus**
*Oh Lord won't you let me, don't you let me*
*Won't you let me wash away the stain*
*Oh Lord won't you let me wash away the stain*

# BIOGRAPHY

County-Galway-born Mary Coughlan has had a varied and chequered career. The eldest of five children, Mary's father was a soldier from Donegal and her mother a housewife from Connemara.

Mary's first memory of singing in front of a crowd was with her sister in an officers' mess at the age of four where she regaled her audience with her own rendition of Bridie Gallagher's 'Two Little Orphans'.

Though she claimed she didn't sing in public again until she was twenty-eight, she has clearly made up for lost time and today cowrites with some of Ireland's greatest songwriters, including Jimmy MacCarthy, Johnny Mulhern and Elvis Costello. The flame-haired Mary has built up a loyal fan base over the years.

Mary moved to the UK in the mid-1970s and immersed herself in family life before returning to her native home and initiating her singing career in 1984, working with Dutch musician Erik Visser, who was to become her long-term collaborator.

An appearance on *The Late Late Show* in 1985 brought recognition, and she recorded her first album *Tired and Emotional*, which fittingly showcased her powerful and bluesy-jazz stylings and became a best-seller in her native Ireland.

She became known for her unique renditions of such songs as the 1948 Peggy Lee hit 'Don't Smoke In Bed', the Billie Holiday ballad 'Good Morning Heartache' and Christy Moore's 'Ride On'.

A woman of many talents, Mary turned her hand to acting in 1988 and appeared in Neil Jordan's *High Spirits*. She subsequently released 'Ancient Rain' and her album, *Uncertain Pleasures*, was recorded in England with producer Peter Glenister. This creation included new compositions by Mark Nevin (Fairground Attraction) and Bob Geldof as well as cover versions of The Rolling Stones' 'Mother's Little Helper' and the Elvis Presley hit 'Heartbreak Hotel'.

At the beginning of the 1990s, Mary signed a new recording contract with Big Cat Records. The label issued an excellent live set and her US debut, *After the Fall*. In June, she presented a series of multimedia shows in Dublin celebrating Billie Holiday, a singer whose life story has some parallels to Coughlan's own. The best of these shows was collected on the wonderful *Mary Coughlan Sings Billie Holiday*. A new studio album, *Long Honeymoon*, was released in April 2001.

Her albums include *Tired and Emotional*, *Under the Influence*, *Ancient Rain*, *Uncertain Pleasures*, *Sentimental Killer*, *Love for Sale*, *Live in Galway*, *After the Fall*, *Mary Coughlan Sings Billie Holiday*, *Long Honeymoon*, *Red Blues*, *Live at The Basement* and a 'Best of' compilation.

*Eleanor Shanley*

## Hard Times

*Written by Steven Foster*

*Taken from the album* Eleanor Shanley and Friends

I have many favourite songs; for various reasons my favourite changes from week to week and varies depending on what mood I'm in. However, my consistent favourite is 'Hard Times'. No matter how often I sing this song, I never tire of it.

'Hard Times' was written by Stephen Foster. He died in 1864 at the age of thirty-seven, having written many great songs including 'Swannee River', 'My Old Kentucky Home' and 'Beautiful Dreamer'. He is buried in Philadelphia and, although born in America, research has shown that he had Irish roots, which would probably account for the connection Irish people have with his songs.

I first learned 'Hard Times' while singing with Dé Danann. Although we never put the song on a Dé Danann album, I did put a live version of it on *Eleanor Shanley and Friends*. This is my favourite version of the song, as it really suits the gospel tradition. The connection between traditional Irish and American gospel was evident when I sang this song with Dé Dannan, and, to me, it is proof that music is a universal language.

Through my work with Self-Help Development Africa, I have been to Uganda and Ethiopia and have seen 'hard times' at first-hand. To stand in the middle of a field in Africa singing 'hard times come again no more' with villagers who have seen little in life but hard times is a real eye-opener. My visits to Africa have given me many things, including a new awareness of the song. Every time I sing 'Hard Times' now, I sing it for the poor, underfunded and ignored people of our planet.

To me, 'Hard Times' is a song that will always have a place in the list of great songs because it is ever pertinent to the 'now'.

## Hard Times

*Let us pause in life's pleasures and count its many tears*
*While we all sup sorrow with the poor*
*There's a song that will linger forever in our ears*
*Oh hard times come again no more.*

### Chorus
*'Tis the song, the sigh of the weary,*
*Hard times, hard times, come again no more*
*Many days you have lingered around my cabin door*
*Oh hard times come again no more.*

*While we seek mirth and beauty and music bright and gay*
*There are frail forms fainting at the door*
*Though their voices are silent, their pleading looks will say*
*Oh hard times come again no more.*

# BIOGRAPHY

A native of Keshcarrigan, County Leitrim, Eleanor Shanley was destined to be a singer, having identified and nurtured a deep love for music.

Her mother's family were all very musical, and her childhood was spent learning songs, which gave her an impressive repertoire from an early age. After she finished school, Eleanor moved to Dublin and worked with FÁS, the state recruitment agency, but maintained a keen and active interest in music and drama, studying with Betty Ann Norton. She also joined the 'Leitrim Wild Roses' Tops of the Town group and performed in various sessions, the most common being in Ned O'Shea's 'Merchant'.

It was here that she was to encounter well-known group Dé Danann, an event that became momentous in her life. Frank Cooney and Ned O'Shea first introduced her to the group, when Dolores Keane had just left the band. Eleanor subsequently met Frankie Gavin and Alec Finn and, just two weeks later, was installed in the band. Eleanor remained with the band for five years and saw the release of two albums: *Jacket of Batteries* and *Half Set in Harlem*.

Additional solo releases for Eleanor include *Eleanor Shanley,* produced by Dónal Lunny, *Desert Heart* produced by Neil McColl, *A Couple More Years* with Ronnie Drew, *Eleanor Shanley and Friends,* produced by Alec Finn and featuring Sharon Shannon, Eddi Reader, Dolores Keane, Johnny Duhan, Dessie O'Halloran, Charlie McGettigan and Ray Lynam, and *Another Day's Journey* produced by John Dunford. She has also collaborated with Tommy Fleming and has the distinction of being the only female singer ever to record with The Dubliners! She is the recipient of John Creedon's radio show 'Most Distinctive Voice Award' and was also nominated for a Meteor Award.

Her most recent album is with Ronnie Drew, *El Amor De Mi Vida* (The Love of My Life). The pair had successfully collaborated a few years back, and is produced by Mike Hanrahan of Stockton's Wing fame.

*Annette Buckley*

## The Ever Changing Colours Of The Sea

*Written by Annette Buckley*

*Yet to be released*

I wrote this song in early 2005. It began as a short poem and eventually turned into a song. I named my debut album after it, which came out in May 2005, although the song itself isn't on it.

I grew up on a farm on the Old Head of Kinsale in the south peninsula of Ireland. It's a remote area and I get all my inspiration from there.

I live very near a cliff top and I can see the sea for miles and miles. One beautiful spring day, I went for a walk. I sat on a cliff edge and began contemplating. The sun shone on the water below and it changed to the most beautiful colours, almost like a rainbow. I thought about death; I had always been afraid of dying, but not that day. I felt alive and free and at peace with myself. I thought that, when I went, I would like to be cremated and thrown in here, in this very spot with these beautiful colours, and laid to rest. 'Let me rest in peace with colours, the ever changing sea of colours.'

It hasn't actually been recorded yet, but I hope to record it during 2006. It is sung in a very slow lament-type style, accompanied by the piano or just with a string quartet. I like the use of these lone instruments; it creates an atmosphere. I usually end my set-list with this song, almost like a farewell, a finale song.

## The Ever Changing Colours Of The Sea

*Me, myself, I seek the vastness of open seas, crazed*
*by power. I only exist, I barely exist.*

*Pick me up by the windfall and lay with me the lasting*
*summer, somewhere, where, no one,*
*Somewhere, where, you'll come.*

*Ah, ah ah,*
*Ah, ah ah,*
*ah ah ah, ah ah ah*

*Let me rest in peace with colours, the ever changing*
*sea of colours,*
*I only exist, I barely exist.*

*Ah, ah ah,*
*Ah, ah ah,*
*ah ah ah, ah ah ah*

## BIOGRAPHY

Annette Buckley first came to prominence via her performances at the Lobby Bar, in Cork and since then she has built up a steady following. Many have witnessed her performances throughout the UK and Ireland, and she has supported both Juliet Turner in her sell-out date at the Cork Opera House and the US-based Ryan Adams at the Kilkenny Rhythm 'n' Roots Festival in 2001.

She has also supported Maria McKee, Nina Hynes, Eleanor McEvoy, Neil Halstead, Amy Rigby and The Soft Boys, and has taken part both in the Forward the Revolution tour in the Village, Dublin, and the 2003 Cork Mid-Summer Festival in the Everyman Palace Theatre.

In 2001, Annette signed a publishing contract with Toby Darling Ltd in England, which offered her the opportunity to exhibit both her voice and her songwriting skills.

In 2004, Annette embarked on a six-month Irish tour, playing piano with Dundalk songwriter Stewart Agnew and collaborating with a number of Cork bands on their debut releases, including Green Monitor, Stanley Super 800 and Rest's debut album *Burning in Water, Drowning in Flame*. It was also during this period that she finished her debut album *The Ever Changing Colours of the Sea,* which was released in 2005.

Jim Pardoen

*Sarah Packiam*

## Homeless Teenage Girl

*Written by Sarah Packiam*

*Yet to be released*

I wrote 'Homeless Teenage Girl' when I was thirteen. I remember looking out the window with my guitar, playing the new chords I'd just learned. My inspiration came from a rose in the garden. It had just lost its last petal – and so my story began, a story almost too dark for a thirteen-year-old. Now, ten years later, I still consider it my best. I wrote with innocence, not knowing how it would change my life.

After winning a 2FM song contest with 'Homeless Teenage Girl', I sang the song live, with my old guitar, on 2TV. I think Dave Fanning gave me an odd look and asked me something about being sad a lot of the time. I found that amusing!

I also recall a journalist asking me if I'd heard of such a story happening in real life – I hadn't. He went on to tell me that it had been in the news, but before I was even born.

So, I've been left slightly superstitious.

Now, sadly, life is all about the 'hits' for songwriters – learning to write and please the record companies who will pigeonhole you, if you're lucky.

I miss that time in my life, when I could write for me.

## Homeless Teenage Girl

*Down a street lit, busy way*
*A sweet little baby and its mother lay*
*Baby just born and all alone*
*Young mother dead*
*She was unknown*

*Chorus*
*And nobody noticed the bundle of joy*
*Or even checked if it was a girl or a boy*
*Just an innocent baby brought to this harsh world*
*Cries for its mother*
*A homeless teenage girl*

*Just like the last petal on the rose*
*Slips off, slides down the stem*
*A vague whimper of a baby*
*As its life comes to an end*
*Last wriggle of its little toes*
*On those tiny cold feet*
*Last pump of its tired heart*
*It struggles at the final beat*

*Chorus*
*And nobody noticed the bundle of joy*
*Or even checked if it was a girl or a boy*
*Just an innocent baby brought to this harsh world*

> *Cried for its mother,*
> *A homeless teenage girl*
>
> *And isn't it crazy its existence so short*
> *A couple of hours never learned to be adored*
> *An innocent baby brought to this harsh world*
> *Cried for its mother*
> *A homeless teenage girl*

## BIOGRAPHY

Sarah Packiam was born in Dublin. She is already a stalwart in the music scene, having worked in music for almost a decade, enjoying great success with 'Homeless Teenage Girl'.

Sarah has been writing songs since the age of twelve and, when she was fourteen, she represented Ireland as the youngest ever contestant in a European radio song contest. On foot of this achievement, she signed a development deal with EMI Ireland.

She now lives in Spain and spends her summers gigging with her family band almost seven days a week.

For the past two years, she has had the pleasure of recording and cowriting with Grammy award-winners Jon Secada and Tim Mitchell.

*Paddy Cole*

## I Wan'na Be Like You

*Also listed as 'King of the Swingers'*
*Written by Richard M Sherman and Robert B Sherman*

We recorded 'King Of The Swingers' when *The Jungle Book* movie came out because it's on that soundtrack, and it's a song that has been synonymous with us ever since. We recorded it about fifteen years ago, and it still goes down very well with the crowd and has become known as our signature tune.

### I Wan'na Be Like You

*Now I'm the king of the swingers*
*Oh, the jungle VIP*
*I've reached the top and had to stop*
*And that's what's botherin' me*
*I wanna be a man, mancub*

*And stroll right into town*
*And be just like the other men*
*I'm tired of monkeyin' around!*

*Oh, oobee doo*
*I wanna be like you*
*I wanna walk like you*
*Talk like you, too*
*You'll see it's true*
*An ape like me*
*Can learn to be human too*

*Gee, cousin Louie*
*You're doin' real good*

*Now here's your part of the deal, cuz*
*Lay the secret on me of man's red fire*

*But I don't know how to make fire*

*Now don't try to kid me, mancub*
*I made a deal with you*
*What I desire is man's red fire*
*To make my dream come true*
*Give me the secret, mancub*
*Clue me what to do*
*Give me the power of man's red flower*
*So I can be like you*

*You!*
*I wanna be like you*
*I wanna talk like you*
*Walk like you, too*
*You'll see it's true*

*Someone like me*
*Can learn to be*
*Like someone like me*
*Can learn to be*
*Like someone like you*
*Can learn to be*
*Like someone like me!*

## BIOGRAPHY

Paddy Cole, the virtuoso sax/clarinetist, progressed from Maurice Lynch's Band to the Capitol Showband and subsequently became bandleader of the Big 8, featuring ex-Royal Showband stars Brendan Bowyer and Tom Dunphy who were resident in Las Vegas at the time.

In the early 1970s, Paddy and his family relocated from the USA to Ireland where he decided to form a new band. Together with Tony Loughman Promotions and breakaway members of the Big 8, The Paddy Cole Superstars were born. Joining Paddy were Mickie O'Neill, Mike Dalton, Michael Keane, Jimmy Conway, Pat Morris, Ray Moore and Twink (Adele King) as lead female vocalist. They played their first gig in the Fiesta Ballroom, Letterkenny, County Donegal, in the summer of 1974.

Through the Superstars, Paddy displayed his versatility and delivered to enthusiastic audiences a melody of tunes – varying from jazz to country, traditional to pop. They boasted a steady and impressive following, so much so that on the back of a successful Canadian tour, the powers that be invited them to settle in Las Vegas. However, they decided to stay true to their Irish roots and returned to Ireland. As time went on, there were many changes, including the departure of some members and the arrival of others, namely brothers Tony and Colm Hughes along with Jimmy Smyth and Micky McCarthy from Castleblaney and bassist Pat Sharkey from Derry.

By the 1980s, many members had gone their separate ways, with Twink carving out a showbiz career for herself as a popular television personality.

Paddy, however, continued to tour the country with his own band, the All

Stars, and they remain hugely popular to this day.

Paddy is also known for the composition of songs, most notably 'The Magee Shuffle', a track written especially for a *Late Late Show* tribute to veteran broadcaster Jimmy Magee. He has also turned his hand to acting and features in the classic film *Hear My Song*, which he lists as one of his proudest professional moments to date.

# A Song That Just Is

*Pat Shortt*

## The Jumbo Breakfast Roll

*Written by Pat Shortt*

*Released as a single*

I can't believe the reaction to 'The Jumbo Breakfast Roll'! They're doing a
new road where I live, like they probably are in every part of the country at
the moment, and every time I went into my local garage there would be a
big queue of fellows looking for their breakfast roll. It was around the time
I was working on my new show, and it reminded me of a sketch I used to
do with D'Unbelievables where a young fella goes into the shop and says,
'I'll have one of them, and one of them and how much are these?' and he'd
be holding up the queue and there would be a girl behind the counter saying,
'Do you want sauce on your roll?'

I knew it was a good piece of comedy, but I couldn't believe the reaction of
the audience when I sang it on *The Late Late Show*. It went very well for me. I
think it was the 2FM DJ Ruth Scott who first downloaded it from the website
and played it on her show, and then Marty Whelan took it then and played it.

So then the audiences started requesting it on all the radio stations, and it turned into a bit of a hit. There were a few factors leading up to this: it had a good tune and it was a good laugh, and I suppose it was January when there was nothing else to listen to on the radio! But I was shocked by the reaction because I really had no intention of bringing it out. So I had to go into the studio the very next week and record it and then it took about three weeks to manufacture it, press it and get it out there.

So it's my first single! I'm working on a few more songs in between *Killinaskully* and touring, so you never know, there might be an album yet!

## The Jumbo Breakfast Roll

*Well I wake up in the morning and I jump straight out of bed,*
*Grab a hold of that luminous jacket and shake that fuzzy head,*
*I don't have time for a fancy breakfast or put muesli in a bowl,*
*I just head to the Statoil garage for the jumbo breakfast roll.*

***Chorus***
*Two eggs, two sausage, two rasher, two bacon, two puddins, one black and one white,*
*All placed like a tower on top of each other and then wrapped up good and tight,*
*If you're having some tea, the milk's over there and you'll find sugar in the bowl.*
*Says she, 'Do you want some sauce on that?' says I, 'I do in my roll.'*

*Well whether you're a chippie or a plumber or a brickie or a team*
*just tarring the road,*
*Or a shower of lads coming home from the razz with a crowd or on your own,*
*If you're working up a ladder or peeling pigs' bladder or find yourself*
*digging in a hole,*
*There's no sight better than melting butter, from a jumbo breakfast roll.*

*Well just the other day after me roll and tea, in me gut I got an awful ache*
*I went to me doctor he said, 'That's an artery blocker you have*
*every morning at break.'*

*So to change my lifestyle he has me walking five miles and*
*seeing a dietician called Noel,*
*But I can't get from my head the sight of two runny eggs*
*on my jumbo breakfast roll.*

*Well the years have passed on and my life has changed and*
*now I am a different man,*
*I have lost three stone, I'm doing a line with a girl called Joan,*
*and we are both vegetarian.*

*My cholesterol is low and my heart is good to go, but in*
*the morning I'd sell my soul,*
*To sit in any Statoil forecourt*
*and devour a jumbo breakfast roll.*

**Chorus**
*Two eggs, two sausage, two rasher, two bacon, two puddins, one black and one white,*
*All placed like a tower on top of each other and then wrapped up good and tight,*
*If you're having some tea, the milk's over there and you'll find sugar in the bowl.*
*Says she, 'Do you want some sauce on that?' says I, 'I do in my roll.'*

## BIOGRAPHY

Pat Shortt was born and raised in Thurles, County Tipperary. He grew up on a diet of Billy Connolly, Niall Toibín and *Hall's Pictorial Weekly* but it was the coupling of Pat and his old friend Jon Kenny in 1986 which provided the perfect ingredients for the hilarious and highly lovable duo that became D'Unbelievables – arguably Ireland's most popular comedy act. Together, they performed their irreverent brand of comedy in theatres all over Ireland, the UK and the USA as well as various countries across Europe. They produced four critically acclaimed sell-out shows along with writing and producing chart-topping videos.

When Jon Kenny became ill in recent years, he was forced to take some time off, and Pat was faced with the prospect of appearing alone in front of an audience for the first time.

Pat has also appeared with the Druid Theatre Company in their production of Martin McDonagh's *The Lonesome West*, as well as in many movies, including *Angela Mooney Dies Again*, *This Is My Father*, and *The Closer It Gets*. He also starred in the 2004 production *Man About Dog*, written by Belfast-born Pearse Eliot.

These experiences were all valuable groundwork for his most recent contribution to Irish television, *Killinaskully*, the first production he has written and produced single-handedly. The comic drama, set in a rural Irish village, has a wealth of diverse and eccentric characters, three of which are portrayed by Pat himself, and the show has been received exceptionally well.

THE YEAR 2006 finds Pat touring the country with his show *You Won't Get Away With That Here*, and the scene is set for fun and frolics amid a range of colourful characters created especially for one run. Set in the village hall which is about to be demolished, we meet Patsy the caretaker who patrols the aisle to make sure that there is nothing unsavoury going on in the back row, Sheamie the builder who comes in to demolish the place, and Dympna the air hostess who lives on in Sheamie's dreams as one of his most memorable conquests.

# *Artists' Websites*

Annette Buckley – www.annettebuckley.com

Anúna – www.anuna.ie

Brendan Bowyer – www.brendanbowyer.com

Brendan Graham – www.brendangraham.com

Brian Kennedy – www.briankennedy.co.uk

Charlie Landsborough – www.charlielandsborough.com

Charlie McGettigan – www.charliemcgettigan.com

Christie Hennessy – www.christiehennessy.com

Christy Moore – www.christymoore.com

Damien Dempsey – www.damiendempsey.com

Declan Nerney – www.declannerney.com

Declan O'Rourke – www.declanorourke.com

The Devlins – www.thedevlins.com

Diarmuid O'Leary – www.thebards.ie

Dominic Kirwan – www.dominickirwan.com

Don Baker – www.donbaker.ie

Eric Bogle – www.ericbogle.net

Eleanor McEvoy – www.eleanormcevoy.com

Eleanor Shanley – www.eleanorshanley.com

Finbar Furey – www.finbarfurey.com

Foster and Allen – www.fosterandallen.com

Gemma Hayes – www.gemmahayes.com

Hazel O'Connor – www.hazeloconnor.com

Honor Heffernan – www.honorheffernan.com

Jack L – www.jacklukeman.com

Joe Dolan – www.joedolan.com

John Spillane – www.johnspillane.com

**Kieran Goss** – www.kierangoss.com

**Kíla** – www.kila.ie

**Leslie Dowdall** – www.lesliedowdall.com

**Liam Clancy** – www.liamclancy.com

**Liam Lawton** – www.liamlawton.com

**Luka Bloom** – www.lukabloom.com

**Marc Roberts** – www.marcroberts.ie

**Maria Butterly** – www.mariabutterly.com

**Marian Bradfield** – www.marianbradfield.com

**Mary Coughlan** – www.marycoughlanmusic.com

**Maura O'Connell** – www.mauraoconnell.com

**Mick Flavin** – www.mickflavin.com

**Mick Hanly** – www.mickhanly.com

**Mike Hanrahan** – www.mikehanrahan.com

**Nina Hynes** – www.ninahynes.com

**Niamh Kavanagh** – www.oldshore.net

**Paul Brady** – www.paulbrady.com

**Pat Shortt** – www.patshortt.com

**Patsy Watchorn** – www.patsywatchorn.com

**Pete St John** – www.petestjohn.com

**Phil Coulter** – www.philcoulter.com

**Rebecca Storm** – www.rebeccastorm.com

**Roesy** – www.roesy.net

**Ronan Hardiman** – www.ronanhardiman.com

**Sarah Packiam** – www.myspace.com/sarahpackiam

**The Saw Doctors** – www.sawdoctors.com

**Seán Keane** – www.seankeane.com

**Shay Cotter** – www.shaycotter.com

**Sonny Condell** – www.sonnycondell.com

**Tommy Sands** – www.tommysands.com

**The Walls** – www.thewalls.ie

# *Permissions*

The publisher and author would like to thank the contributors for their co-operation and permission for the reproduction of lyrics and would also like to thank the following for permission to reproduce copyright material:

'A Time for Love' lyrics by Paul Francis Webster. © Warner Bros Inc. Lyrics reprinted by permission of Alfred Publishing Co. Inc • 'Lost Inside of You' written by Barbara Streisand and Leon Russell © 1976 First Artists Music Corp. Lyrics reprinted by permission of Alfred Publishing Co. Inc • 'A Time to Learn' written by Pat Alger & Tim O'Brien © 1993 PolyGram International Music Publishing Inc, USA (37.5%)/Forerunner Music Incorporated (31.25%) /Howdy Skies Music (31.25%)/Rondor Music (London) Ltd (62.5%)/Universal Music Publishing Ltd. (37.5%). Reproduced by permission of Music Sales Ltd. All rights reserved. International Copyright Secured • 'Make Me An Island' words and music by Albert Hammond & Michael Hazelwood ©1998 Shaftesbury Music Company Ltd. Chrysalis Music Ltd. Reproduced by permission of Music Sales Ltd. All rights reserved. International copyright secured • 'The Old School Yard' written by Patsy Cavanagh © Bardis Music Ltd. Reproduced by kind permission of Bardis Music Ltd • 'The World Is What You Make It' written by Paul Brady © Hornall Bros Music Ltd. Reproduced by kind permission of Hornall Bros Music Ltd • 'Absent Friends' by Duncan McCrone and Cy Jack © Jammy Music Publications. Reproduced by kind permission • 'Dublin In The Rare Auld Times' written by Pete St John. Reproduced by kind permission • The Magdalen Laundry written by Johnny Mulhern. Reproduced by kind permission • 'The Hucklebuck' written by Andy Gibson and Roy Alfred © 1948, 1949 Bienstock Publishing and Quartet Music, Inc. Copyright renewed. Lyrics reproduced by kind permission of Carlin Music Corp, London NW1 8BD • 'We Will Fly' by Charlie McGettigan and Audrey Healy © Rattlesnake